DEAF TARGET

Peter Jackson

First published in Great Britain 2002

Copyright © Peter Jackson 2002

Published by
Deafprint Winsford
PO Box 93
Winsford
Cheshire CW7 3FU
ENGLAND

British Library Cataloguing Data

ISBN 0-9532206-4-8

Printed in Great Britain by Palladian Press Limited, Unit E, Chandlers Row, Port Lane, Colchester, Essex CO1 2HG

Other Crime Books by Peter Jackson

Deaf Crime Casebook
Deaf to Evidence
Deaf Murder Casebook

History Books

Britain's Deaf Heritage
A Pictorial History of Deaf Britain
A History of the Deaf Community in Northwich and
Winsford 1880-2000
(With Maureen Jackson)
Deaf Lives (Ed.with Raymond Lee)
Manchester Memoirs (Ed.)

For Wayne

Contents

Introduction

This book differs from the first three on deaf crime in that it concentrates on deaf people who have been murder victims, whether by other deaf people or by hearing people, rather than deaf people who have killed.

It may be surprising to find that very few deaf people have actually been murdered by hearing people, or by serial killers, unless the murder was gang-related or sexually motivated.

There are only three known deaf victims of serial killers, and two of the stories are described here (though one of the 'serial killers' does not meet the criteria as he was arrested before he could kill more people). The other serial killing victim is the unsolved murder of a deaf prostitute, one of a series of at least 8 other prostitutes.

There is only one known deaf victim of a poisoner and that story is also described here. It would seem poison is not a favourite method of killing deaf people!

There are also few known instances of deaf persons being murdered in mafia-style shootings. This is uniquely Russian and also reported in this book.

In contrast, there have been dozens of reported attacks on deaf sign language users by gang members who mistook the sign language being used for other gang-signs or offensive signs. Some of these attacks have had tragic consequences for the deaf people involved, as stories in this book show.

However, most deaf people are killed or murdered by other deaf people. Two stories here from Chicago and Australia illustrate how the criminality of certain Deaf people is directed at their own community. Both resulted in a killing, because the criminals had no choice. To leave the victims alive would be as good as putting themselves in jail because they could be identified.

Finally, we have the South African case of Clive Michael. This must be unique in the annals of Deaf crime. This is also an unique **_police_** crime.

I leave the reader to discover the book and hopefully enjoy it.

Peter W. Jackson
February 2002

Chapter 1

1871: Hull, England

Lust that ended in Murder!

Quite a few present-day centres or institutes for adult Deaf people were, in the period 1850 to 1880, also used for the education of local deaf school children. Most of these classes were small and were attended by children on a day-to-day basis and were usually taught by one schoolmaster. The Deaf and Dumb Institute in Dock Street, Hull, Yorkshire was one such establishment that had a small class of deaf children.

The Dock Street institute appears to have been unfortunate with its choice of schoolteachers. In 1870, the then schoolteacher was dismissed for misbehaviour towards some of the schoolgirls and the Committee of the Deaf and Dumb Institute advertised for a new schoolmaster. They received a response from Charles Sleight who had sixteen years experience as a schoolteacher at the Brighton Institution for the Deaf and Dumb, where his brother, William, was still headmaster. The Sleight family had, and were to have, a long association with the Brighton Institution, ending with Arthur Sleight in the 1930s. One of the Sleight family, the Reverend Blomefield Sleight, was elected the first president of the British Deaf and Dumb Association in 1890.

Charles Sleight's credentials impressed the Committee at Hull and he commenced his duties as schoolteacher in November 1870. From the first, his cheerful manner endeared him to the local Deaf people who attended meetings at the Institute and he appeared to be an excellent teacher, having a good rapport with the children in his charge.

Until he could get a place of his own, Charles Sleight lodged with a deaf couple, John and Maria Hailstone in rooms above the Deaf Institute, where Maria acted as housekeeper, preparing meals for the schoolchildren and generally keeping the premises tidy. Both were former pupils of the Yorkshire Institution for the Deaf and Dumb at Doncaster, John being several years older than Maria who was aged 22 and by all accounts a pretty young woman.

By day, John Hailstone was a journeyman painter employed by the local firm of Messrs. Stainforth and Son at Paragon Street, Hull, where he had been employed for 13 years and was then earning a good wage of 24 shillings. In consequence, for much of the time during the day, Maria Hailstone and Charles Sleight were thrown together by their respective occupations within the Deaf and Dumb Institute.

By early March, it was known that Charles Sleight was "walking" with a young lady from Brough, near Hull, a Miss Jacques, and was saving and buying furniture with a view to marriage.

At the same time, however, it was clear to a number of people that Sleight was not his usual self. The secretary and treasurer of the Hull Deaf and Dumb Institute, Thomas Haller, who was on good terms with

Sleight thought he was depressed and attributed this to money worries. He recommended that Sleight should seek medical treatment and referred him to a Doctor Macmillan who first saw Sleight on 20 March. When Dr. Macmillan had to go out of town for a few days, he passed the patient onto another doctor, Dr. John Wilkinson who was also incidentally the local police surgeon.

"I would be pleased if you could keep an eye on him," Dr. Macmillan told the other doctor. "I have some concern he might be losing his reason."

Dr. Wilkinson said that he would look in on Sleight first thing on Monday morning.

Around the same time, Maria Hailstone informed her husband that Charles Sleight had pulled her down onto his knees.

"He kissed me. More than once," she said.

"Kissed you?"

"Oh, it were nothing. It were just play," Maria said.

John Hailstone, who knew that Maria was fond of their lodger, thought the whole episode had been of a playful nature and laughed it off.

On Saturday night 25 March, Charles Sleight approached Thomas Haller at the conclusion of a social evening of adult Deaf people and requested that they had a serious talk. Haller promised to call at the Institute between 12 noon and 1 p.m. the next day so that Sleight might talk to him about what was troubling him.

When Haller went into the Deaf Institute the next morning, he found Charles Sleight sitting on the sofa in an exceedingly nervous and excitable state. Sleight held the Bible in his hand and had been reading from it before the appearance of Haller, who thought that the schoolteacher appeared to be greatly troubled. John and Maria Hailstone, together with Maria's brother George Guest, who was also Deaf, were all also present in the room.

"Do you think there is any forgiveness for great sinners?" Sleight asked Haller.

The secretary and treasurer asked the schoolteacher to say what was troubling him. Sleight said that if Haller would come and sit up against him, he would tell Haller, as he had always been his confidant. Sleight told Haller that he had been recently exceedingly tempted.

"Tempted to what?" asked Haller.

Sleight said that he had been thrown together alone with Maria Hailstone so much that he had been tempted and had taken Maria into his arms and kissed her. Haller told him to drive all such impure thoughts out of his mind. To get him out of the house, Haller invited him over for tea later that afternoon. This was not an uncommon occurrence because the teacher had tea with Haller on two of the preceding four Sundays.

On this occasion, Sleight arrived at approximately three o'clock in the afternoon and immediately asked for Haller's bible, from which he read some portions. Under questioning by Haller, the teacher told him that he was positive he had not committed fornication with Maria Hailstone. She had not come onto him in any way, but he was experiencing deep feelings for her because of her beauty and because she was around him in the house so much. Haller counselled him to put these feelings out of his mind because of his engagement to Miss Jacques.

Upon leaving Haller's house after tea, Sleight asked if his host would be calling into the Institute that evening. Haller thought not, as he had been there that afternoon but said he would look in first thing in the morning.

That evening, Charles Sleight led the evening prayers and addressed the small gathering of local Deaf people for several minutes before retiring up the stairs to his room for the night at about ten o'clock.

The premises at No. 10 Dock Street was a three-storey building, with the Hailstones occupying the top floor, Sleight the middle floor and the meeting rooms were on the ground floor. After the last Deaf person had left the Institute at 10.30 p.m., John Hailstone went on his rounds locking and fastening all the doors and windows. The front door had a latch which had to be manually locked with a key and all the occupants of the Institute had one. Having satisfied himself that all was secure, John Hailstone retired to bed, passing Charles Sleight's bedroom door, which was shut. His wife, Maria, had earlier also retired and was asleep on the side of the bed furthest from the door.

In his evidence given at the inquest, several members in the audience laughed or smiled when John Hailstone stated that he had "heard" no noise coming from Charles Sleight's bedroom during the night. Just at that very moment, the Town Hall clock struck five o'clock, and seeing the disbelieving smiles on the audience, John Hailstone told them that he could hear the clock striking! Apparently, John could hear and speak a little and was not totally deaf.

The next morning, John Hailstone awoke at 5.40 a.m., and telling Maria it was half-past five, left her in bed going back to sleep. He dressed quickly and quietly and made his way downstairs to the scullery where he had a quick wash, opened the kitchen shutters, then let himself out of the house by the front door, leaving it fastened by the latch and made his way to the station where he caught the 6 a.m. train to Hessle where he was working at that time.

Only two people know what happened in the next hour but it is safe to assume that John Hailstone was not as quiet as he said he was in getting dressed or washing himself in the scullery. Charles Sleight waited until Hailstone had left the house and made his way upstairs quickly to the Hailstones' bedroom where Maria Hailstone was still asleep.

Perhaps Sleight thought that with her husband out of the way, Maria Hailstone would allow herself to be seduced; perhaps Maria Hailstone, in her sleepy state, thought it was her husband coming back to bed because she allowed her nightdress to be removed, leaving only a flimsy chemise and one stocking. It seems clear that once she realised it was NOT her husband who was in bed with her and removing her clothes, she resisted strongly. As stated at the inquest, the prevailing opinion of Maria Hailstone as a person was that she was kind, cheerful, affectionate and perfectly chaste.

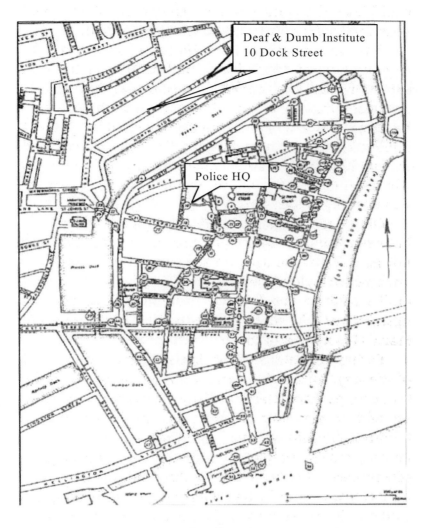

Deaf & Dumb Institute
10 Dock Street

Police HQ

Map of Hull, c1875,
showing location of Dock Street
and Parliament Street

Perhaps Sleight misinterpreted Maria Hailstone's kind and affectionate manners and the way she had allowed him to kiss her. Perhaps he thought she might prove willing so when she started to struggle and tried to fight him off, it enraged him. Whatever it was, Charles Sleight lost all reason and produced a razor blade he had brought with him and slashed wildly at the unfortunate woman, almost decapitating her.

Sleight then calmly got dressed and walked to the Central Police Station in Parliament Street. On duty in the charge room was Police Inspector William Grace who was just getting dressed. It was just after seven o'clock that Inspector Grace noticed the man, whose name at that time he did not know, come through the slightly open charge room door.

"I want to see the Superintendent," Grace heard the man say.

"What do you want, sir?" Inspector Grace asked.

"I want to see the Officer-in-Charge."

"I am that person."

Up till then, the man (who was Sleight) was calm and rational, as any person would be in asking a question, but upon Inspector Grace saying he was the person in charge, Sleight came round the counter to the middle of the room where Grace was standing.

"There has been a young woman murdered in Dock Street," Sleight informed Inspector Grace

"Where?"

"At the Deaf and Dumb School, No. 10 Dock Street."

"How was it done? Who has done it?"

In answer, Sleight held out his left hand, which the inspector saw was bloodied and there was a cut. There was something wrapped round the hand, which appeared to be a white rag with blood on it.

"Did you do it?" Sleight was asked.

"Yes, I did it."

Grace then pointed to a chair and told Sleight to sit down, which he did. Up till then, Sleight had been perfectly calm, but immediately he sat down, he jumped up again, waving his arms excitedly and tried to seize some papers on the desk and got one of them ready to tear up, but Grace snatched it away from him. He then attempted to seize a ruler which was close to him. Again, Grace stopped him, only for Sleight to turn round and snatch a poker out of the fireplace. Grace got it away from him and bundled him into the reserve room. Grace called out to the reserveman (jailer) who was getting the overnight prisoners washed and breakfasted. In Sleight's presence, Grace told the reserveman what had been said, but Sleight continued to act in a violent manner and appeared to be insane. The two officers could not keep him quiet, so another officer was sent for and the three of them managed to get Sleight into a cell where he was searched.

The police officers found on Sleight the sum of £22.10.0 in gold, along with five £5 notes, three shillings and two pence in other coins. Also found on the prisoner were two small penknives and a bunch of keys.

Parliament Street, location of Kingston-upon-Hull
police station and police court where
Charles Sleight was arrested.

Sleight was charged with being in an unsound state of mind in a Police Station, a temporary measure designed to allow the police to detain him whilst they carried out enquiries.

Leaving a man at the cell door to guard and keep an eye on the prisoner, Inspector Grace went to Dock Street. On the way, he met a police constable on patrol and asked him to accompany him to the Deaf Institute. Grace rang the front door bell several times without getting a reply, then tried the passageway door leading into the kitchen. This door opened a little way before being stopped by the chain inside which held it fast. Examining the latch keyhole, the inspector noticed it was a very small one and upon recalling seeing a small key on the bunch of keys taken from the prisoner at the police station, he went back there and obtained the keys.

On his second visit to No. 10 Dock Street, Grace was accompanied by a different police officer, Sergeant Thompson and found that the key he had identified at the station did indeed open the front door. Together, the two police officers examined each room as they went through each floor. On the top floor, Grace found the door leading to a bedroom open a little way and there was a key on the inside of the door. Although the window blind was down, he could see a bed in the room between the door and the window. On the bed, there was a sheet which had a large stain of blood a little way down from the pillow about where the chest of a person would be if lying in the bed. The bedclothes were partly off the bed on the far side of the bed next to the window on the floor, and going round to the far side of the bed, Inspector Grace discovered the body of a woman.

Maria Hailstone was lying partly on her left side with her face to the boards, with bedclothes partly under her and partly over her. However, the lower half of her body was uncovered. A pillow resting on the body against the bed was saturated with blood and the wall between the bed and the window was also stained with blood as was the lid of a clothes box that lay under the window. Lifting up the bedclothes from the body, Grace found that her head had nearly been cut off although the body was still warm. The woman's hands and arms were covered with blood, and there was a large pool of blood under her legs.

Inspector Grace sent Sergeant Thompson out to get the Police Surgeon, who arrived between 8.15 a.m. and 8.30 a.m. His on-scene examination deducted that the cause of death had been due to a large haemorrhage and convulsion following decapitation. The Police Surgeon, Dr. Wilkinson, estimated the time of death as between 1½ and 2 hours earlier. The body was then removed to the morgue at the police station for further examination whilst Inspector Grace continued his examination of the murder scene.

In the deceased's bedroom, Grace found a razor still wet with blood and going down the stairs to the next floor, he found on the steps at the bottom of the stairs some bloodstains. In the lower floor bedroom (subsequently proved to have been Sleight's), the inspector found a washbasin with the water red with blood and two towels marked C S slightly stained with blood. On the dressing table, he found five razors and a cutting stone which was still wet with oil, denoting recent use.

On returning to the police station, Inspector Grace went to the prisoner's cell and charged him with killing and slaying a young woman at the Deaf and Dumb School. Upon examining the prisoner's clothes, he found no blood stains, but on the underdrawers, he found a large stain of blood on the left knee. These were taken off him and given to Dr. Wilkinson for forensic testing.

On a subsequent return to the murder scene, Inspector Grace discovered wrapped up in a travelling rug a nightgown saturated with blood, subsequently identified as the deceased's.

A subsequent autopsy by Dr. Wilkinson confirmed that the cause of death had been by the slash on the throat from behind the right ear across to the left ear which had severed all the structures in the front of the throat. The instrument used (the razor) had penetrated the vertebrae in two places on the spine as if an attempt was being made to cut off the head. There were other superficial injuries to the left shoulder and on the hands where the deceased had tried to ward off the blows. The autopsy found that there had been no violent penetration of the vagina.

Following enquiries, the police traced Thomas Stainforth, John Hailstone's employer, and brought him to the police station where he identified the body as Maria Hailstone, the wife of his employee. Immediately, Stainforth (who could communicate with John and his late wife in sign language) set out for

Hessle where he told the unfortunate man what had happened to his wife.

John Hailstone left his place of work immediately and went to the police station, his mind in a state of complete shock. He could not believe that Sleight had gone so far as to murder his wife. He had known Sleight was fond of Maria, but to kill her? If only he had heeded the warning signs when Maria first told him Sleight had kissed her, but neither had taken it too seriously.

At the inquest, the coroner's jury learnt that a number of people had noticed the odd behaviour of Charles Sleight in the days immediately preceding the murder.

"Even the mutes observed it and mentioned it. They thought his mind affected and made the signs indicating that opinion," Thomas Haller informed the jury.

The coroner's jury returned a verdict of "Wilful Murder" against Charles Sleight after hearing evidence presented.

Charles Sleight was taken from the Borough Prison to the Kingston-upon-Hull Police Court in the Town Hall on Friday 31 Match 1871 for the magistrates' hearing. As he was being conveyed in a hansom cab by two police officers, Sleight was alleged to have made a number of comments to the two officers.

"Oh, is not this a very bad job?" he said just as they left the prison.

Charles Sleight—

POLICE COURT
Borough of Kingston-upon-Hull,
TO WIT.

Stands charged before me, the undersigned, Her Majesty's Stipendiary Police Magistrate, in and for the said Borough this *4th* day of *April* 1871, for that h *e* the said *Charles Sleight* did, on the *27th* day of *March* 1871, at the said Borough. *feloniously wilfully and of his malice aforethought did kill and murder one Maria Hailstone against the peace of Our Lady the Queen Her Crown and Dignity and —*

~~of the Monies, Goods and Chattels of~~ _____ ~~then and there being found feloniously steal, take, and carry away~~, contrary to the form of the Statute in such case made and provided, and the said charge being read to the said *Charles Sleight —* and the witnesses for the prosecution

Thomas Bashley Stainforth, John Hailstone, John Wilkinson, Thomas Haller, William Grace, William Murdock, and Thomas Bartholomew —

being severally examined in h *is* presence, the said *Charles Sleight*

is now addressed by me as follows:—" Having heard the Evidence, do you wish " to say anything in answer to the charge ? You are not obliged to say anything " unless you desire to do so, but whatever you say will be taken down in writing, and " may be given in Evidence against you upon your trial."

AND I, the said Magistrate, stated to the said *Charles Sleight* and gave h~~im~~ clearly to understand that he had nothing to hope from any promise of favour, and nothing to fear from any threat which might have been holden out to h~~im~~ to induce h *er* to make any admission or confession of h *is* guilt, but that whatever ·he should then say might be given in evidence against h *im* on h *is* Trial, notwithstanding such promise or threat. Whereupon the said *Charles Sleight —* saith as follows :

I have nothing to say

The charge sheet at Kingston-upon-Hull police court

17

A little further on, he said, "Oh, she was such a nice girl. Oh, what a state her father and mother must be in. They must be in very great trouble about it. I don't know what could possess me ever to do such a thing."

The police court heard evidence from John Hailstone, interpreted by Thomas Stainforth, that Charles Sleight had resided with him and Maria for about four months since he had moved up from the Brighton Institution. The first month had been at their previous residence and they all had moved into 10 Dock Street about three months prior to the murder, with Maria giving up her employment as a dressmaker to assume the duties of housekeeper to the institute and to Sleight. As far as he was aware, there had not been any trouble or passion between Maria and their lodger. They had, however, noticed some eccentric behaviour from Sleight over the preceding two weeks.

Charles Sleight was committed for trial at York Assizes where, on 4 April 1871 at the direction of the judge, he was found Not Guilty on the grounds of insanity and directed to be kept in strict custody until Her Majesty's pleasure be known - in other words, confined to a mental institution.

Chapter 2

1902: Dour, Belgium

Bloodbath at the Farm!

For much of his 31 years, Charles Audez had a reasonably sheltered life. Born Deaf without speech in the small Belgian town of Dour approximately 7 kilometres from the French border on 13 March 1869, he was sent to the Mons School for the Deaf to receive an education.

On leaving the school, an apprenticeship as a general handyman/farm labourer was found for him on a farm belonging to a family named Harmignes on the outskirts of Dour. This position was thought to be most suitable for him as the Harmignes family had a deaf daughter, Marie, a few years younger than Charles, who was also attending the deaf school at Mons.

For the next few years, Charles helped out on the Harmignes family farm and his close proximity to the deaf daughter, Marie, enabled a close relationship to be formed between the two after Marie in her turn left the school at Mons. It seemed to everyone in Dour and the surrounding area that the two Deaf people were suited to each other and that they would eventually marry. Being able to communicate with each other in sign language helped to foster the growing relationship, which was encouraged by the Harmignes parents who had no other children and no doubt saw their farm eventually being taken over and worked by the Deaf couple. Charles Audez was regarded as a hard worker, very orderly in his work and also saved his money well. Marie's father was well satisfied with him.

But all was not well within the Harmignes farm. The farm was hard work and offered little prospect to Charles Audez who began to chafe at the restrictions under which he was placed. As he turned 30 years old, he began to resent the idea that everyone had his life mapped out for him – marriage to Marie followed by years of likely hand-to-mouth existence to try and make a living out of the farm.

His resentment at his circumstances began to fester like an ulcer within him, and there was no doubt that Marie Harmignes and her parents began to worry about Charles' state of mind and his intentions towards her. It was obvious that he was starting to avoid being left in the company of Marie, and spoke to her less and less, becoming melancholy and moody.

Charles Audez's resentment exploded just before 6 a.m. on the morning of 25 February 1902. It had begun as a normal working day, with the two women starting work in the kitchen whilst the father went out into the barns to attend to the livestock. Charles had already milked the family's small herd of goats and cows and had come back into the house for a wash.

The two Harmignes women working in the kitchen looked up as they saw Charles enter the room and their smiles of welcome gave way to gasps of horror as they spotted the heavy calibre 9 mm revolver in his hand. They barely had time to scream before Charles Audez raised the revolver and fired.

The first bullet struck the mother in the chest, and she fell dead, the bullet having ruptured her heart.

Marie Harmignes turned and tried to run out of the room, pursued by her fiancé. Two bullets missed their target but two further bullets hit her. The first struck her in the side of chest, almost blowing away her breast; the second struck her in the upper jaw.

As she fell seriously wounded, her father rushed into the room. He had been outside but had been startled by the shooting. He was horrified to be greeted by the carnage in the kitchen, his wife dead spread-eagled on her back on the floor, and his daughter also down, bleeding profusely. He only had time to take in the fact that Charles Audez was standing in front of him with a smoking gun before the revolver barked once more, and the father went down, shot in the abdomen.

By the time the police arrived on the crime scene, summoned by neighbours who had heard the shooting, Charles Audez had gone. As the hunt began for him, both Marie Harmignes and her father were taken to the hospital at Mons where surgeons operated to try and save their lives.

Le père Harmignes died in the hospital at 5.30 p.m. later that same evening. The heavy calibre 9 mm bullet had done too much damage to his internal organs for the surgeons to be able to save him. They were more successful with Marie Harmignes, stabilising her condition so that over the next week she was able to improve and move out of danger.

It was not until the following afternoon, 26 February, that the police were able to pick up traces of Charles Audez' flight. They traced him to the French border village of Henzinnes, thence to Condé sur l'Escaut where he caught a train heading for Paris. After that, the trail went cold.

On Friday morning, 7 March 1902, at approximately 10 a.m., a coalminer named Parez was walking through a glade in a wood named Cocars, outside the village of Elouges about two kilometres from Dour when he spotted a body. After ascertaining for himself that the body was dead, he reported his discovery to the police in Elouges.

The mayor and commissioner of police of Elouges accompanied the coalminer back to the body. The two men recognised the body as that of Charles Audez. They saw that Audez had shot himself in the right temple with a revolver found in his right hand. There was another loaded revolver inside his jacket pocket, together with at least 50 bullets. Charles Audez had apparently left the Harmignes farm with his life savings, because there was a wad of notes in his pocket amounting to over 100 francs.

The post-mortem conducted by Dr. Pernet, police surgeon at Elouges, found that Audez had been dead for at least a week. It was apparent that with nowhere really to go, and having a feeling of being pursued by the police, he had returned from the French border to the area where he had grown up and committed suicide.

No one, not even Marie Harmignes when she fully recovered from her injuries, was able to explain why Charles Audez had acted in such a manner.

Chapter 3

1929: California, USA

The Wife Who Liked To Have Fun

Standard, in California's Sierra Mountains, was typical of many places that had experienced a boom as prospectors flocked to the region in search of gold. However, in the 1920s some of these places had gone into decline and were little more than ghost towns. Evidence of California's Gold Rush still showed its scars all over the mountains. Nowadays, though, much of the work was connected with the timber industry and Standard had a timber mill. In this timber mill, there worked a young man named Carroll Rablen, who lived with his widowed father, Steve.

Carroll Rablen had become totally deaf in World War I when a German shell had exploded in his dugout in France and by the mid-1920s, he was a lonely man yearning for female company. To put it bluntly, he wanted a new wife, full stop. He had been married once before, but the marriage had barely lasted a year before his wife left him.

In order to meet eligible females, he had started writing to women whose names he had been given by a marriage agency. In the past few months, he had written dozens of letters without getting any joy.

He was now writing another letter when a shadow fell over the table where he was writing. He looked up and saw that the shadow belonged to his father.

Steve Rablen waited until his son was watching his lips before he spoke.

"I suppose you're writing to that matrimonial bureau again."

"Well, Pa. There's this woman's name in Texas they gave me."

"Texas!" his father snorted. "What you want to be looking for a woman in Texas for? What's wrong with our California girls?"

"We've been over this before, Pa," his son replied. "You know there's no woman in Tuolumne County who'll have me."

"I know that but I sure wish you'd forget the whole idea. You don't need a wife. You've got me."

That was precisely the point. The first marriage had collapsed because his wife could not stand it any longer putting up with his father so Carroll Rablen ignored his father's disapproval and posted off the letter. A few days later, Eva Brandon Young was reading the letter in Quanan, Texas. She liked what she read. She was broke, with a son of 11 years whose father had died when he was just a month old. The land round her home was flat, brown and lifeless and she liked the idea of living in the California Sierra Mountains. She responded to the letter, sending a picture of herself.

When Carroll Rablen showed the letter to his father, Steve Rablen frowned darkly.

"Why, she's a widow with a little boy. What you want to be saddling yourself with a young lad for? You oughta get a single woman, if you must write these letters."

"So she's been married before! I don't mind that," his son said.

"She looks like an Indian," his father said desperately, trying to make his son change his mind. It was true that Eva had part-Cherokee blood in her.

"So what? There were some Indians in my army company. They were all good fellows. You could trust them anywhere."

"Well, I don't like it. Tell her that. I don't wanna you marrying a woman with a kid. I don't like it, see?" The finality of the tone was the echo of a lifetime's dominance over his deaf son.

This time, however, Carroll Rablen was not prepared to let his father interfere in his marriage like he had done with his first marriage. He wrote back to Eva Young and told her he still wanted to meet her but warned her of his father's disapproval.

Eva Young wrote back promptly: *"...if I don't suit your father, so what?..."*

That decided Carroll Rablen. Eva Young caught a train from Texas with her 11-year-old son for San Francisco, and Carroll Rablen came down from the mountains. They met for the first time on 12 November 1927 at San Francisco's railroad station and drove to Reno where they were married the same day.

From the start, Eva Rablen and Steve Rablen did not get on. He resented any intrusion to the bond between himself and his son and went out of his way to make her life as miserable as possible. There were heated rows when Eva gave back as good as she got.

"I wish you'd leave here," Steve Rablen said during one row, not for the first time.

"I came here with my husband," Eva would shout back, "If he wants me to go, he'll say so."

The situation was not helped by two factors. One was that Carroll Rablen had suicidal tendencies. He was broody and often depressed. Eva had once dissuaded him from one suicide attempt and those suicidal tendencies had also been part of the reason why Carroll's first wife left him.

The second factor was the dislike felt for Eva in the surrounding community. Women in small settlements are wary of strangers. Perhaps it was her Cherokee blood that caused the dislike, perhaps it was the way the marriage had taken place. Most people in Standard viewed the marriage as a bit too unconventional and did not approve of Eva.

Perhaps it was also the way Eva danced at the weekly dances in Tuttletown, a few miles away from Standard where regular Friday night socials were held in the ramshackle old schoolhouse where men in high boots and gaudy shirts glided over the crowded floor, dancing with women in gay calicos. People came from all over Tuolumne County to these dances. They came on foot, on horseback, in whole families by wagon. There were many lonely lumberjacks down from the timber camps restlessly searching for stray women.

Eva Rablen was popular with the men at these dances. They would watch her and compete for the opportunity to dance with her. Eva danced as the Cherokee dances, with rippling, sensuous movements that left men filled with desire.

In one corner of the dance hall, two grey-haired fiddlers would saw away at their violin strings. For years, Tuttletown relied on these two men to provide the music for their regular dances. The violin players were Steve Rablen and his brother John, Carroll's uncle, and Steve Rablen would grit his teeth in anger as he watched his detested daughter-in-law flit over the dance floor.

On the night of 26 April 1929, a special dance was being held to mark the end of the long winter season. As usual, Carroll Rablen sat alone in his dilapidated car parked just outside the open doors of the dance hall, watching the dancers inside. He never took part in these dances because he could not hear the music. He only came to these socials because his young wife loved dancing. He did not know why he really stayed to watch the dancing, because inside, he was tormented by the sight of his wife whirling around in the arms of many different men. Perhaps he stayed because he preferred to bring his wife home from the dances himself, rather than entrust another man to do so. It was clear that many of the men inside the dance hall would take advantage of any situation that presented itself, perhaps with the willing participation of Eva herself. So, Carroll Rablen would grit his teeth each week and drive his wife to her regular dances and watch her enjoy herself whilst he patiently waiting in the car outside smoking cigarette after cigarette so that he could drive her back home himself.

From time to time, Eva Rablen would come outside to the car and ask her husband if he was alright, and if he wanted to go home. Each time, Carroll Rablen would tell her to go back inside and enjoy herself.

The dance continued and the evening passed quickly – at least for those inside. For the lonely man outside, the evening continued to be one long wait. As midnight drew near, the tired fiddlers played the closing number "Kiss Me Goodnight". Eva Rablen snatched a plate of sandwiches and a steaming cup of coffee, and zigzagged through the dancers to the door, intending to carry them to her husband. As she drew near to the door, she bumped into another young woman who was whirling about in the final waltz, nearly spilling the coffee.

"Oh, pardon me!" exclaimed Eva Rablen.

"Think nothing of it," said the other.

Rablen and his wife exchanged a few words as he ate the sandwiches. Before he drank his coffee, Eva Rablen started back to the dance floor, trying to get one final dance before the evening was over.

Suddenly, a scream reached the dancers above the noise of the music and dancing, which stopped abruptly. People inside the hall could see that Carroll Rablen had slumped in his seat, writhing in agony. Men and women ran out to the parked car. One woman jerked his collar open while another ran for water. Two men tried to lift him out of the car but were stopped by others. Elbowing their way through the crowd came the two violin players, Steve Rablen and his Uncle John.

"Speak to me! What's the matter?" Steve Rablen shouted at his son.

Eva Rablen   Carroll Rablen

The young man stared at him with glassy eyes, struggling to speak. Finally, he gasped, "The coffee! It was bitter..." then there was no more response.

The nearest telephone was half a mile away. By the time someone had ridden his horse to it and summoned the doctor, Carroll Rablen was dead.

The little town was mystified. There was little opportunity for excitement in the town, and now the residents made the most of it. Word of Rablen's death spread rapidly. Men and women were on the streets, talking in excited little groups, and of course gossiping about the Rablens as they had done many times before.

By the time Sheriff Dampacher of Tuolumne County reached the scent, together with his deputies and the coroner, Mrs. Josie Terzich, the schoolhouse had become the centre of a grim investigation. Questioning of Eva Rablen, her father-in-law and of all those who had been at the dance began at once whilst the body was taken away for a post mortem and an analysis of the contents of the stomach.

From the start, the widow became the central figure in the enquiry as, between sobs, she related the events leading up to her husband's death. She said she could not understand what had happened and thought that perhaps it had been a stomach attack, as her late husband was sometimes prone to them.

"Did he go with you willingly to the dance?" the sheriff asked.

"Of course, he always did," the widow was quick to answer. "He liked to come and never minded waiting in the car outside. He didn't dance because he couldn't hear the music. Carroll came back deaf from the war, you know. He had been sort of unhappy and broody about that lately, feeling out of things."

"Brooding and unhappy," the sheriff interrupted. "Do you think maybe it was suicide?"

Eva Rablen shook her head, "It's possible but I doubt it very much."

Rablen's elderly father, weeping and near collapse, was equally puzzled. So were the people of Tuttletown as one by one they were interviewed. However, it appeared from what they were saying that they did not feel too friendly towards Eva Rablen. Some referred to her sarcastically as the "mail order bride". Although no one questioned could shed any light on the death, most were happy to talk to the sheriff's deputies and offer gossip, including the fact that Steve Rablen detested his daughter-in-law.

Police officers who searched the car to try to find any evidence that would support the theory of suicide could not find anything. Even Carroll Rablen's clothing yielded not a single clue, and there was no note of any kind.

"Perhaps it was not suicide at all," the sheriff said. "Perhaps it was just natural causes."

"We will have to wait for the post mortem," the coroner decided. However, when Mrs. Terzich performed the autopsy, it failed to disclose the cause of death, and the analysis of the stomach contents – on which so much hope had been pinned – was equally disappointing. No trace of any poison was found.

Sheriff Dampacher was determined to press on with the inquiry, and one day Steve Rablen dropped into his office. By this time, the aggrieved father had the sympathy of the entire countryside. He had idolised his son and now he was inconsolable. Since Carroll's death he had sat alone for hour after hour in his rundown cabin out on Blanket Creek where he had been born.

"I know why you have come, Steve," the sheriff said. "Let me tell you I have not given up on this case. It's just that we have not found the answer yet, and we can't rule out suicide or natural causes."

"Suicide! That's a lie! My boy didn't kill himself," snapped the old man. "And he didn't die from no stomach ache either. Like I told you, he spoke a few words to me before he went and he told me the coffee was bitter. No sir, he didn't kill himself. I'll take a bet on that, and I'll tell you something else. Carroll was murdered and I'll tell you who done it – his wife!"

"That's a very serious charge!" the sheriff told him. "We haven't any evidence at all."

Steve Rablen, the embittered father of Carroll Rablen, who hated his daughter-in-law, pictured together with Carroll's uncle John and the insurance policy that they believed was the motive for the murder.

"I'll tell you why. For his insurance and I'll tell you something you don't know. Every time she read of some feller being killed, she'd say to Carroll, 'I wonder if his wife will get the insurance.' I've even heard her say she was sorry she ever married my boy."

It was evident from the way Steve Carroll talked that he had never liked Eva Rablen, and now his dislike had turned into hatred. The sheriff finally promised that he would question Eva Rablen again but warned the father that he could not do anything without credible evidence.

He decided to search the schoolhouse once more, and early the next morning, he was standing in exactly the same spot where Carroll Rablen's car had been. The ground around it had been searched time and time again, but this time the sheriff began from scratch, determined to be as thorough as possible. Using his position as a radius, he moved out slowly, pawing away leaves and debris. He dug into the soft ground. Every inch came under his scrutiny and still he found no trace of anything. It looked like a hopeless task. For more than an hour the search went on, doggedly and relentlessly. At last he came to the schoolhouse stairs. Suddenly his eye fell on a broken board over the second step, and he saw an open space under the staircase. He had no recollection of having observed it before. Obviously he had overlooked it.

He went down on his knees, thrusting his arm into the opening. His hand groped to right and left. Then suddenly his fingers caught the feel of something hard and smooth. He pulled it out – a little bottle. And on its face he saw a label. One look and he felt his pulses pounding. The word on the label, printed in heavy type, was *Strychnine*. But it was not until long afterward that he was to learn how that bottle came to be there.

When Dampacher looked more closely he found that the label, in small type, bore the name of the Bigelow Drug Store in the little town of Tuolumne, a few miles away. It did not take him long to get into his car and make for the pharmacy. Warren Sahey, clerk in the Bigelow Store, greeted him at the door, sensing at once that this must be a serious visit.

"Look over your poison register for me – quick," the sheriff asked, handing Sahey the bottle. "I want to know who bought this and when. And remember, not a word about this to anybody, do you understand?"

The druggist opened his record book, running his finger down the lines of recent purchases. Soon he stopped abruptly. "Here it is," he said, "this was bought here on the afternoon of 26 April."

The sheriff nodded, trying to conceal his excitement. It was the afternoon before the fatal dance. "Now then, tell me who bought it."

"A woman – she signed the name of Mrs Joe Williams and I remember now, she assured me she want it to kill gophers, otherwise I wouldn't have sold it to her without a doctor's order."

"That helps," said Dampacher. "Now, one thing more. Could you recognize this Mrs. Williams if you saw her again?"

"Naturally," the other answered. "I always take a good look at customers when they come in with prescriptions or to get anything with poison in it. Part of my business, I guess."

The sheriff admonished him again to keep silent. "I'll be back in a jiffy with a woman. Take a good look at her but don't say a word. Then I'll come back here and I'll be alone."

It did not take the sheriff long to reach Mrs. Rablen's home in Tuttletown. He found her sitting at her window and she waved to him as he approached. She did not seem low-spirited.

"Come, take a little ride with me," he suggested. "A few things I'd like to talk over with you. We'll be right back."

Soon afternoon Dampacher pulled up in front of the pharmacy in Tuolumne. The young widow seemed unconcerned but the sheriff, surmising that it might be difficult to get her into the store, already had thought of a ruse. "I need a cake of soap," he told her. "Come on in with me and we'll get a soda. We can both stand one on a warm day like this." He took her arm and escorted her into the place before she could even think of objecting.

Twenty minutes later they were back in the car and had resumed a casual talk about Rablen's death. Arriving at the widow's home he said good-bye rather casually and she hurried in.

Sahey, the drug clerk, was standing outside the store, an excited look on his face, when the sheriff returned. "That's the woman," he blurted. "That's the woman who bought the poison. I could pick her out of a hundred dames. But - say, isn't she Mrs. Rablen?" Dampacher quickly put his finger to his lips and Sahey knew exactly what that meant.

In a short while Mrs. Rablen heard a knock on her door. "You back again, Sheriff?" she greeted her caller with apparent surprise. "Come in."

Dampacher wasted no time. "Tell me something, Mrs Rablen," he demanded. "Why did you buy a bottle of *strychnine* at the Bigelow Drug Store?"

The woman stared at him with a look of blank amazement. "Me buy a bottle of *strychnine?* I haven't bought any thing like that in my whole life."

"Let's have the truth this time," the sheriff snapped, his voice raised. "Why did you buy *strychnine* and why did you use the name of Mrs. Williams? Answer me that – now – and don't lie."

Again she shook her head. "It's not true. It's a lie. I didn't buy poison no place and no one can say I did. And if you're trying to say I bought poison to kill Carroll with, that's a lie, too, and I can prove it."

Sheriff Dampacher dropped a heavy hand on her shoulder. "The man in that store just identified you. He's positive you're the woman who bought the poison – the woman who used the name of Mrs. Williams. That's enough for me. You're under arrest."

Mrs. Rablen smiled. "What a joke. How can that jerk say I bought poison when I didn't? And why should he be able to remember every face that comes in his shop? Anyway, I'm innocent. You'll regret this, Sheriff."

District Attorney C. H. Grayson was sent for from his office in Sonora, the county seat. He was amazed at the news they gave him, but his own investigation had led him to suspect the wife. He believed she wanted her husband's insurance. There were two policies totalling $3,000 in her favour.

They brought the widow in again but she parried every question, brazenly and defiantly. It's all a pack of lies," she repeated. "My father-in-law's behind all this. He never did like me – and now he's getting even. You'll see."

Grayson and the sheriff sent for the aged father and told him of the latest turn. Demanding justice, he swore to a formal complaint charging his daughter-in-law with the murder of his son. But the law enforcers realized too well the weakness of their case. In their own minds they were satisfied of the woman's guilt, yet they realized their limitations. They understood that their case, being only circumstantial, had to be strong and foolproof. And they conceded that it still was weak, especially since the chemist had not found poison in Rablen's stomach. Theirs was a real dilemma.

The officials had read of the remarkable performances in other cases by a research chemist named Heinrich that had helped to solve several other mysteries. Now, after the failure of their own efforts to find poison in Carroll Rablen's stomach, it was decided to send for him. He was their last hope if the case was to be cleared up properly.

On the next afternoon Heinrich arrived in Sonora. The sheriff, the district attorney and their men were closeted with him for hours, going over every detail, answering his many questions. Together they traced all of Mrs. Rablen's movements – or at least all those they know – from the moment she reached the dance hall with her husband. Heinrich listened eagerly, puffing hard on his pipe. As they were nearing the end of their story and were relating Mrs. Rablen's walk through the dancing crowd with a full coffee cup in her hand, Heinrich rose suddenly from his chair. Something had captured his imagination and, as it later developed, he was following that strange intuition which so often guided him.

"Let me get this right," he asked slowly. "I want to be certain that I understand it all. The floor was crowded, you say. People were dancing and she walking through that moving, jostling crowd holding a cup of hot coffee in her hand. Is that what you say took place?"

Heinrich's mind was working fast and soon he and the sheriff were working out plans for a new line of inquiry, one that had not been thought of before. On its results they all pinned high hopes.

Before Heinrich prepared to leave he asked the coroner to give him the contents of Rablen's stomach. He did not ask who had made the earlier analysis or by what method it had been done, being concerned only with his own tested procedures, which he wished to follow in his own laboratory. He did explain, however, that to make a conclusive search for poison, it was extremely necessary to analyse every bit of the stomach contents and to utilise the most modern extracting devices with specially prepared glassware, as well as accurate instruments which he said he kept in his laboratory for work like this. He also took with him the poison bottle, some of Rablen's clothing and other items. And before he left they all agreed that his entry into the case should remain a guarded secret for the time being, at least. Should he fail, the defence might use the fact to good advantage in freeing Mrs. Rablen.

Days slipped by with the authorities waiting anxiously for word. From Mrs. Rablen and her friends came louder protests of her innocence and rumours of mysterious new evidence they said would prove her guiltless. She had engaged C. H. Vance as her attorney. He announced at once that it would be easy to clear his client and that every claim of the prosecution could be countered. Rablen was a suicide, he maintained, and he could prove it.

Tuolumne County was by now divided – some strongly behind the widow, others certain that she was a murderess. Feeling was running high. Everywhere in northern California the case was a main topic of conversation. News and rumours came from many quarters. The county paper carried little else. One day a relative of Mrs. Rablen announced that he had located the real Mrs. Joe Williams who had bought the poison. The next day a Mrs. Crawford, a neighbour of the Rablens in Standard, came forward with the first intimation that Mrs. Rablen would claim an alibi.

"Mrs. Rablen was at my home the exact hour she is supposed to have bought that *strychnine*," Mrs. Crawford was quoted as saying, and she implied that she had witnesses to support her story. Others advanced new reasons for Rablen's suicide. One declared he often had said life wasn't worth the struggle, that he was $1,000 in debt and could not live on his $80 monthly wage.

With growing confidence the defence announced that it had engaged detectives to prove clinching points although its case was in airtight shape.

Meanwhile, through long days and nights, Heinrich was working in his laboratory, his role in the case still a secret. Surprises came in quick succession. First he made a phone call to the sheriff and told him he had subjected Rablen's stomach contents to all known tests. As a chemist, he was skilled in these procedures, having handled many cases in which evidence of poison was difficult to detect.

"There are very definite traces of *strychnine* in the stomach," he reported. "It took a time to find them but the traces are there – unmistakably."

That was the first development. The next came through the plan that Heinrich had evolved in his earlier talk with the sheriff. He had reasoned, reconstructing Mrs. Rablen's movements, that it was logical a suppose that the woman, making her way across a crowded dance floor with coffee in her hand, might have collided with a dance. In that case, coffee – only a few drops perhaps – could have spilled. Heinrich always based his calculations on the natural laws of possible happenings. On that supposition, Sheriff Dampacher had renewed his interrogation of every person known to have been on the floor at the time. Of these he asked these questions:

"Did you see Mrs. Rablen carrying coffee to her husband? Did she bump into you? If not, did you see her colliding with anyone else?"

It was a long, discouraging procedure. Negative answers were coming fast. Dozens of people had been interviewed to no avail. And then, at last, Dampacher found the answer he was seeking. It came from a young woman, Mrs. Alice Shea. It was she who had told Mrs. Rablen, after their collision on the dance floor, to "think nothing of it." Both had taken the words literally – far too literally, in fact.

"Yes, I remember bumping into Eva at the dance," she told Sheriff Dampacher. "It was dark and Eva bumped into me as I came up the steps, She spilled a little coffee on my dress but.."

"She did *what?*"

"Spilled some coffee on my dress," said the woman, slightly surprised at the sheriff's reaction. "It wasn't anything serious but.."

"Never mind," the sheriff interrupted impatiently, "where's that dress now?"

"Home, of course. It's not been washed yet."

"Get it right away and bring it to me," Dampacher directed.

The dress, with a few coffee stains, was sent at once to Heinrich. In his laboratory the coffee stains spoke the words that the law had needed.

"I can give you a definite report now," Heinrich phoned the sheriff. "I've finished my tests on those coffee stains on the woman's dress. As I surmised, they show definite traces of *strychnine*."

The scientist still was far from finished. "I need something more from you," he told Dampacher. "Have one of your men drive that Rablen car up here to my laboratory. There are a few things I want to do with it."

They already had examined every inch of that machine, but they knew that Heinrich had his own way of doing things.

A few days later he was at the telephone again. "I've got more news for you. A few drops of coffee splashed from the cup to the car upholstery. I've analysed them, too, of course. As you probably can guess, they also show *strychnine*. And that cup I asked you for, the one he drank from, there were minute dregs stuck to the bottom. I found them by using the microscope. They show the same poison."

Heinrich now faced one more task, for it was necessary to link Mrs. Rablen still more definitely with what now had been revealed as murder. That task taxed another of his versatilities; from chemistry he turned to his skill as a handwriting expert. He had the poison register from the Tuolumne pharmacy, the one with the signature of "Mrs. Joe Williams." With it he had taken a number of specimens of Mrs. Rablen's

41

handwriting. At quick glance they appeared dissimilar. Heinrich felt that the Williams signature showed awkward signs of disguise, however. Following usual procedures, he photographed individual letters in each, enlarging them to enormous size. With minute care he measured loops and strokes, comparing their size, their form, the depth of ink impressions.

A week later he appeared at the sheriff's office, carrying bulky charts covered with letters in heroic size. "I have my written report for you here," he said, "but you can easily see for yourselves. The handwriting is identical."

Heinrich's part in the case still remained a secret but there were rumours that the state had "something big up its sleeve." The newspapers mentioned it. Just what it was no one seemed to know.

In her cell in the old county jail, built in the fifties when the law was the gun that each man toted, Mrs. Rablen met all interviewers, apparently more confident than ever, insisting she was sure of vindication and that only suicide could explain her husband's death.

Her attorney was even more confident in spite of the latest rumours. "I can say one thing to you now," he told newsmen. "This case will never go to trail. If Mrs. Rablen had wanted to poison her husband she could have found better opportunities for doing it – and safer ones, too – than in front of a crowded dance hall."

"But what about the *strychnine* bottle from drug store?" someone pressed.

"She didn't buy that – and we will prove that, too."

May 13, the day for the accused woman's preliminary hearing, came at last.

Never at the height of the gold rush had there been such a day in the Mother Lode country. From early morning crowds of men and women came flocking from miles around to another of California's picturesque ghost towns, Columbia, in the heart of the Mark Twain country. Some came in broken-down machines, others in trucks and on horseback. A party of high school girls arrived in a chartered bus. Everyone wanted a glimpse of the first woman ever to be accused of murder in the colourful history of Tuolumne County.

Judge J. W. Pitts stepped from his house an hour before court was to convene. He took one look at the crowded streets and he knew that his little courtroom on Shaw's Flat was not the place to hold the hearing. He realized that he had a problem on his hands and one that called for quick thinking. To exclude from his courtroom all but the few it could hold would bring indignation. So he quickly ordered court set up in an open-air dance pavilion near the heart of town. The crowd gathered fast. No court in California ever had a more picturesque or a more bizarre setting. For courtroom walls huge granite boulders towered. Tall pines stood about as silent sentinels.

A hush fell over the throng as Judge Pitts walked to an improvised desk at one end of the dance floor and announced that court was in session. The hearing was under way, but those who came for sensations soon were disappointed. From the start it was obvious that this would be only a routine procedure because both

43

sides were determined to withhold their evidence until the actual jury trail.

A few witnesses told what they had seen of Rablen's death and of events immediately preceding it. Everyone knew that. Sheriff Dampacher related his finding of the poison bottle, and the chemist identified Mrs. Rablen as the purchaser. There was drab testimony by the coroner and a few others. District Attorney Grayson closed the hearing with brief statements.

Then Judge Pitts asked Mrs. Rablen to stand and he ordered her to be held for trial in the superior court. "Is that all?" someone in the courtroom exclaimed, half aloud. There were disappointed faces everywhere.

Eva Rablen (arrowed) in the unique open-air court in Sonora, California.
The judge decided his court was too small to cater for the thousands who came to see the 'Borgia of the Sierras'.

Smiling confidently, Mrs Rablen was led away and, guarded by deputies, driven back to the jail in Sonora. The crowd lingered, strolling in leisurely fashion through the streets. It was like some strange new holiday. But no one knew what they were celebrating.

Suspense ran high through the days that followed. The Rablen case continued as a conversation piece, with the countryside more divided than ever. Bitter arguments were frequent.

On May 17 Mrs. Rablen appeared before Superior Judge J. T. B. Warne in Sonora and entered a formal plea of not guilty. Her trail was set for June 10. There was less than a month to wait.

New developments continued coming in quick succession. There was the finding of a new state witness, his story making front-page news. H. C. Brown, an insurance man of Oakdale, volunteered that the day before Rablen died he complained that he could not pay another life insurance premium. His policy would have to lapse.

Then, to the surprise of everyone, Rablen's first wife appeared. Now Mrs. Frank J. Grandon of Stockton, she said she was convinced that he had killed himself.

"It's his father," she told reporters. "He dictated to him all the time. There was jealousy, bickering and uncontrollable rages. I had to leave. I couldn't stand it."

Carroll had often told her he would be better off dead. Once, she said, he told her he had thought of throwing himself into the machinery of the lumber mill where he worked. The defence exulted.

On all sides, the opening of the trail was awaited tensely. Women were counting off the passing days. Nothing like this ever had occurred before.

Then, suddenly and unexpectedly, the secret of Heinrich's entry into the case leaked out, just how no one knew. The newspapers everywhere gave it headlines. His reputation as a master crime detector was recalled. Just what he had accomplished here no one but the prosecution knew. Yet the word spread fast that he had solved the case, and that he had all the answers.

The big surprise came early in the morning of June 4, less than a week before the trail date. Defence Attorney Vance walked unexpectedly into Judge Warne's courtroom. He stepped briskly to the bench and whispered to the judge. No one in the handful of lawyers and court attendants sensed the meaning of his few words.

An hour later a deputy sheriff walked into the nearly empty courtroom. Mrs. Rablen was at his side. Lawyers eyed each other, dumbfounded.

The bailiff rapped for order. Mr. Vance rose to his feet.

"Your Honour," he began, as the few in seats leaned forward, cupping their ears for every word. "If Your Honour please, my client would like to change her plea."

Eva Rablen, already dubbed by the press as the 'Borgia of the Sierras' had known that she now stood no chance after having learnt of Heinrich's work and rose to her feet.

Judge Warne stared at her in amazement. "Is this true?"

The woman nodded.

"Yes, Your Honour, I – I plead guilty."

The words fell like a bombshell.

"That plea may mean life imprisonment or hanging for you," the court advised her sternly. "Do you still want to make that plea?"

Again she nodded and her attorney asked that sentence be pronounced at once.

"Then," said the man behind the bench, "it is the sentence of this court that you be committed to the state prison at San Quentin for the remainder of your life. I have spared you from the death penalty on condition that you never be paroled and that your sentence never be commuted. This court stands adjourned."

Trembling, Mrs. Rablen was led away. Once back in jail she related how she had bought the poison and had given it to her husband in the coffee. She said she had thrown the empty poison bottle under the schoolhouse stairs, feeling certain that it never would be found. She even claimed that Rablen, wishing to end his life, had asked her to give him poison; but this phase of her story the authorities dismissed as fantastic, for they were convinced that it was only a last-minute thought in the faint hope of arousing sympathy and trying to excuse her crime.

On June 10 she entered San Quentin Penitentiary smiling apparently indifferent to her fate.

"Now I'll have enough leisure," she said, "to do what I've always wanted to do."

47

"And what's that?" a guard inquired.

"Study Spanish."

Less than an hour later she exchanged her name for Number 47180.

Chapter 4

1983: Chicago, USA

Sign Language Mistaken for Gang Signs

One of the few urban legends which have an element of truth in them are the occasions when Deaf people, communicating in hand signs, have been threatened, injured or killed by assailants who mistook the signs for gestures of threat or disrespect. This happened to a young deaf man named Freed who was driving along a road in Stockton, California (about 30 miles east of San Francisco) one evening in 1993 when their car was overtaken by a 16-year-old-driver whose 15-year-old passenger misinterpreted the signing as a gesture of disrespect and fired at Freed's car, killing him outright.

In Los Angeles on 12 February 1994, a young woman was shot in the face when communicating with her boyfriend as they drove to dinner. Seven young men, believed to be gang members, in a truck driving alongside opened fire after misreading the signs. She was lucky. She survived. Not so lucky were two deaf brothers who were blasted off their motorcycle in a Los Angeles parking lot by a spoilt rich young man. (*See Chapter 6 for the story*).

A year later, in February 1995, 20-year-old Latell Chaney lost an eye after being beaten by five Minneapolis teenagers who allegedly took his signing to a friend as gestures inviting a fight. Matthew Tebow, also aged 20, was unluckier at a party in Detroit in September 1996. He was shot and killed after his signs to a deaf friend were misinterpreted during a brawl that erupted at the party.

Even an innocent sign language conversation with deaf friends on the pavement could have dire consequences. A Chicago man was shot and wounded on 26 July 1998 after a passing car full of teenagers misinterpreted their signs whilst in Beirut, Lebanon, a group of Deaf Arabs signing on a street corner during the civil troubles were fired on by a Militia unit, killing one of them and wounding the others. In Croatia, Bosnia and Kosovo, there were several incidents where deaf people signing to each other were mistaken for the opposition and shot at, killing some and wounding others.

However, for an extreme example of sign language being mistaken for gang-style signs, we go to Chicago where at 9 p.m. on 5 March 1983 a 25-year-old Deaf black male named Carey Epkins got himself lost in an unfamiliar neighbourhood on his way to a party.

Spotting three young women standing outside a store on the corner of Cermak Road and Kolin Avenue in the west side neighbourhood of Lawndale in Chicago, Epkins stopped his car and got out. Whilst standing with his door open, he attempted to ask the three girls by using gestures and sign language directions to where he wanted to go.

However, the gestures and sign language used by Epkins apparently perplexed the girls and they shouted to two men lounging nearby for help.

Seeing the two men approaching, Epkins raised his hands in a shrugging motion, which was misinterpreted by the two men as the sign of a rival gang. One of the men punched Epkins in the face, which served to knock him backwards through the open door of the car, dislodging the brake. Epkins attempted to drive away but the two men rushed into the car after him. In the violent struggle inside the car, Epkins hit another car at the intersection, and then made a U-turn, heading west in the eastbound lanes.

Witnesses reported hearing three shots being fired during the short drive before the car came to a stop half a block away in front of a restaurant at 4351 W. Cermack Road.

The two assailants jumped out of the car and fled, leaving Epkins slumped over the steering wheel. Diners in the restaurant called the police and the paramedics, and Carey Epkins of 1336 West 14th Street, Chicago, was taken to Mount Sinai Hospital with three wounds, one in his chest and one in each leg. He was pronounced dead after emergency surgery at 10.10 p.m.

Questioning witnesses in the vicinity, police soon identified the two men as members of a local gang named Joseph Brownlee and his cousin. It was clear that it was the cousin that had struck the punch that sent Epkins crashing back into his car, but Brownlee, aged 18, was the man witnesses had seen running away from the stalled car holding a gun.

Brownlee was soon arrested and charged with the murder of Carey Epkins. His cousin gave himself up to Detective Thomas Lazar of the Harrison Area Violent Crimes Unit and agreed to testify for the prosecution in return for immunity.

Joseph Brownlee stood trial before Judge James M. Bailey in the Cook County Criminal Court on 20 October 1983. Assistant State's Attorney Richard Schwind argued that under a relatively new piece of Illinois legislation that allowed longer sentences to be imposed if the victim was handicapped, and the handicap made the victim unable to prevent the crime, Brownlee was eligible to receive a prison term longer than the usual maximum of 40 years.

"If the victim could talk," Schwind argued before the court, "he would probably still be alive today."

However, Judge Bailey noted that Brownlee had no prior convictions and declined to impose an extended term sentence, ruling that Brownlee must go to prison for the maximum of 40 years.

Chapter 5

1987: Chicago, USA

Tied Up and Suffocated!

When a family member contacted social work staff on Monday 16 November at Thresholds, a private rehabilitation agency in north Chicago, to raise her concerns over a relative who had not contacted her for over a week and had failed to turn up at a weekend family get-together, the staff checked with those who were in charge of the agency's Bridges Program. This was a project that was being funded with public money for deaf people who were former psychiatric patients.

Bridges Program staff confirmed that the last time they had seen Linda Sanborn was on Friday 6 November when she had joined other project users for lunch.

"She missed lunch all last week, and also an important review appointment with the psychiatrist," her caseworker told the relative. "We thought she was ill and could not let us know."

"But she has a TTY," the relative said. "Being ill before never stopped her using it before. She always comes to us for Sunday lunch and would have let us know if she could not make it." *[TTY – deaf telephone device.]*

Social work staff agreed with the relative that the matter needed to be investigated. The caseworker was detailed to go with the relative to the one-bedroom apartment at 5010 N. Hermitage Avenue on the top floor of a three-storey courtyard-type building. After receiving no answer to their repeated ringing of the front doorbell, which was connected to a flashing light that would warn the occupant of someone at the door, the caseworker and relative went downstairs and found Juga Kale, who said she was the manager of the building, waiting for them to find out what was wrong.

The caseworker explained that they were concerned for a resident who had not been seen for over a week.

"Come to think of it, I haven't seen Linda since the weekend before last either", the manageress said. She agreed to back upstairs with them and use her master key to open the front door.

Unfortunately, a security chain was in place and preventing their entry.

The three women could also smell an odour coming from the apartment and suddenly fearful, they decided to call the police.

The first officers on the scene broke the security chain to enter the apartment and found that it had been ransacked. After viewing a body on the bed, the officers decided a homicide had also been committed and called the Belmont Area Violent Crimes unit who sent a squad under the command of Lieutenant Michael Malone to take charge of the investigation.

Linda Sanborn, who was 25-years old, was found face down on her bed, fully clothed. Her hands and feet were bound with twine. There were no obvious signs of trauma but her body was discoloured and it was obvious she had been dead for a number of days. An autopsy conducted by the Cook County medical examiner would later determine the cause of death as asphyxiation and there were signs that she had been subject to an assault as there was a large bruise on her jaw. However, there were no signs that she had been sexually assaulted.

Deaf since birth with poor speech, Linda Sanborn had a deprived childhood. Her parents wanted nothing to do with her and there were also suspicions that she had been sexually abused within the family. This led to her being made a ward of the State of Illinois when still in her early teens and to her being adopted as a teenager. It was her adoptive mother who had gone to the Threshold rehabilitation centre with her concerns.

As a psychiatric patient, she had worked on placement sporadically within the community in jobs found for her by the rehabilitation centre and her last employment had been a three-month stint as a kitchen worker in the Ponderosa Restaurant in the Niles area of Chicago. She had finished this placement in September and was waiting for another placement at the time of her murder. She had only been living independently in her apartment since April that year.

Lieutenant Malone told reporters that there were no signs of forced entry to the apartment. "It wasn't a burglary type entry," he said.

"She admitted someone that she knew to the apartment, or that someone had a key to the front door," Malone's statement went on.

Malone confirmed that the victim had been dead over a week when the body was discovered and admitted the police did not have any suspects or motive at that moment, but they were questioning neighbours and checking her movements within

Chicago's Deaf community. Their inquiries found that she belonged to several Deaf social groups and regularly played in one Deaf bowling team.

Neighbours within the apartment complex told detectives that another Deaf girl had shared Linda's apartment for about a month but had moved out in late October following constant rows.

Manageress Juga Kale said the two girls had been warned about their behaviour and the noise of their rows. Most of these arguments stemmed from the other girl regularly having male visitors to the apartment and taking advantage of Linda's simple nature.

Lieutenant Malone refused to be drawn on whether police were seeking suspects who were themselves members of Chicago's Deaf community but in a significant development, he requested that a police officer named Daniel Levin be attached to his investigation team in order to question Deaf friends and acquaintances of the deceased.

"Officer Levin is able to use American Sign Language and has a wide knowledge of Chicago's Deaf community," Malone said in a press statement. "He will be an asset to the team because the deceased was deaf and speech impaired."

The evening of the same Monday that the body had been discovered, Officer Levin accompanied detectives to a house in the Park Ridge area of Chicago where they questioned two Deaf women living there. One of these women was the former roommate of Linda Sanborn. They recovered from the apartment a TTY, a television set, a set of bar lights and other items subsequently identified as belonging to Linda Sanborn. The two women in the house told Levin that these items had been left in the apartment by their boyfriends.

A police computer check found that Linda Sanborn had lodged a complaint with the police in August that year complaining that a Danny Lord and a Scott Nilsson had punched her in the face while stealing some things from her apartment. Police had not even bothered to investigate the complaint against the two men, who were the boyfriends of the two girls.

After the interrogation of the two Deaf girls, who were not charged with possession of stolen goods, police officers arrested two men separately at their homes and brought them to the Belmont Area squad offices where they were interviewed in sign language by Levin.

2 charged in slaying of woman

Like victim, suspects are deaf and speech-impaired

By Philip Wattley
and Andrew Martin

Two deaf and speech-impaired men were charged Tuesday with the murder of a Ravenswood neighborhood woman, also with speech and hearing impairments, who was killed during a burglary in her home.

In a police interview conducted in sign language, the suspects, Danny J. Lord, 22, of 1654 N. Fairfield

Nilsson

Lord

then questioned by Officer Daniel Levin, who specializes in working with speech- and hearing-impaired persons. Police determined that Lord's girlfriend was Sanborn's roommate until she moved out Oct. 21 after a disagreement.

Lord and Nilsson went to Sanborn's apartment late Oct. 8 and began looting the woman's home while she slept, police said. Sanborn woke up during the home invasion and was attacked by the two men,

Chicago Tribune article announcing the arrest of two Deaf men for the murder-burglary of Linda Sanborn.

As a result of statements made during those interviews, Danny Lord, aged 22, and Scott Nilsson, aged 20, were charged with the murder of Linda Sanborn.

Scott Nilsson had no previous convictions, but Danny Lord was known to the police. In March 1984, he had been arrested on burglary charges and sentenced to three years probation. He was also fined $70 in court costs.

According to a police spokesman, the two men admitted obtaining a key from Sanborn's ex-roommate that fitted the apartment front door and using it to burgle the place on Sunday night 8 November.

Linda Sanborn had been asleep lying fully clothed on her bed when the two men disturbed her. She sat up and switched the bedside light on. However, before she could scream or struggle, she was punched hard in the face which caused her to fall back onto the bed, unconscious. The two burglars then bound her feet and hands together and ransacked the apartment.

Apparently, police said, the victim recovered consciousness during the burglary and recognised the burglars.

Knowing that the victim would refuse to remain silent about the second burglary and that they would face a prison term if the victim went to the police like she did during the first one, the two burglars decided to silence her. As Nilsson held the struggling girl face down on the bed, Lord pushed her face into a pillow until her life expired.

The two men escaped the apartment by exiting through a window, leaving the front door on the security chain to delay discovery of the body.

"The victim was simple-minded and had psychiatric problems," Lieutenant Malone told reporters. "These two men made her life a misery for months, constantly stealing from her and taking advantage of her. They treated the poor girl very callously, knowing that she had difficulty in communicating her problems to other people. They killed her to shut her up but they made too many mistakes."

"They admitted punching her and pushing her head into a pillow," a police spokesman later told reporters. "She apparently suffocated."

Legal arguments in pre-trial hearings delayed the start of the two defendants' trials for over 18 months as the defence attorneys and the District Attorney's office contested the way police had obtained statements from Lord and Nilsson without the presence of a sign language interpreter. It was alleged that the statements were obtained after an interrogation conducted by Officer Levin in sign language when the proper procedure should have been to have a qualified ASL interpreter present.

Defence attorneys also questioned whether use of Officer Levin in the police interrogations breached the defendants' Miranda rights. They argued that Levin's familiarity with Chicago's deaf community put Nilsson and Lord at a disadvantage and lulled them into a false sense of security resulting in them making statements that incriminated them.

The legal manoeuvrings resulted in plea bargains that saw the two men have separate trials at Cook County Criminal Court. Danny Lord's trial was the first to take place, in June 1989, when he was given a sentence by Judge James Bailey of 60 years in prison.

Scott Nilsson's trial took place in the same court in December 1989 when he was sentenced to 35 years in prison for his part in the murder and burglary of Linda Sanborn.

Chapter 6

1990: Los Angeles, USA

Blasted off their Motorcycle!

Brothers Cesar and Edward Vieira were very close, brought even closer by their deafness. They were both Deaf from birth; both married to Deaf women and went to the same school. The two deaf brothers and their wives lived in the same house with their families and attended the same church, which offered sign language services. They lived in an environment where the use of sign language was a dominant factor in their daily lives.

Born in Rio de Janeiro, Brazil, Cesar was brought to the United States at the age of 3 when his mother emigrated. Edward was born in Los Angeles.

Both Cesar and Edward attended Birmingham High School in the Van Nuys area of Los Angeles. This was a mainstreamed school with a deaf/hearing-impaired unit attached. It was there that Cesar met his future wife, Delores.

Although Cesar could speak, though not very well, Edward's efforts at speaking were so poor that even his mother could not understand him so wherever possible, the brothers communicated in sign language.

Cesar and Delores had two children, and Delores was expecting their third child at any moment. She was nine months pregnant.

Edward and his wife also had one child, and the two families lived together in a house in the remote

Antelope Valley desert in the fast growing suburb of Palmdale, 60 miles east of Los Angeles.

Cesar trained and qualified as a motor mechanic after leaving school whilst Edward worked at a variety of jobs. He was currently a drywall installer.

On Sunday 28 January 1990, the two brothers decided to pay a visit to their mother and other brother who lived in the Los Angeles suburb of Reseda. Because of Delores' imminent pregnancy, she elected to stay at home with the children and her sister-in-law also stayed to keep an eye on her. Instead of using their car, the brothers therefore decided to do the ride on Edward's Kawasaki 600 motorcycle.

After a pleasant meal with their mother, Berenace Cree, and middle brother, Marco aged 29, the deaf brothers left on the motorcycle to drive the 60 miles back to their home, with Cesar riding pillion as Edward drove.

As they were driving through the San Fernando Valley, they came to a traffic light at the junction of Devonshire Street and Balboa Boulevard where they came to a halt at the red light. The brothers were communicating in sign language whilst waiting for the light to change when they observed a two-door, light-blue Hyundai hatchback pull up alongside them. The group of youngsters in the car appeared to be making obscene gestures at the two brothers who stared back at them.

When the light turned green, Edward gunned the motorcycle forward but the Hyundai caught up with them and started crowding them towards the edge of the road until the brothers were forced to pull into the parking lot of a J. C. Penny store near the San Fernando shopping centre to try and escape the car.

However, the Hyundai followed them into the parking lot, and two young men jumped out from the front seats of the car. To the brothers' horror, one of the teenagers was waving a gun.

Apparently, some of the teenagers in the car did not even know that there was a gun going to be used. They were simply looking for a fight, and when the gunman fired the first shot, which grazed Cesar Vieira, they started yelling: "No, don't shoot!" but the other kid reloaded his gun and kept firing.

Cesar Vieira was blasted off the pillion of the motorcycle, hit in the chest. Edward Vieira, who had dismounted in anger to confront the teenagers for crowding him off the road, was hit in the hip and the shoulder and fell where he stood. Then the car's driver walked over to the Kawasaki motorcycle and casually kicked it.

Because it was a two-door hatchback, some of the teenagers in the car had not even got out of the car. Now, a 17-year-old girl who was originally a passenger scrambled into the driving seat and started to gun the car forward as the two assailants scrambled back inside and the car tore off the parking lot and headed towards the San Diego Freeway.

"I smoked him! I smoked him!" the teenage gunman was yelling.

"What the hell did you do that for?" some of the others yelled back at him. "We were only supposed to have a fight!"

"I should have shot him in the head and killed him!" the gunman shouted back.

"Idiot!" one of them shouted at him as realisation started to dawn on them they were in serious trouble.

The gunman retorted: "Why should we all go home with bruises and blood all over us when I made it simple and easy!"

Back at the parking lot, shocked bystanders started to converge on the fallen deaf brothers to help them. Cesar Vieira lay on his back on the tarmac bleeding to death whilst Edward struggled to understand what had happened. It was also some time before the helpers realised both victims were deaf.

Cesar was taken to the Holy Cross Hospital where surgeons tried unsuccessfully to save his life. He was pronounced dead at 1 a.m. on Monday morning, 30 January, five hours after the shooting had taken place at the shopping centre.

Police struggled to find a sign language interpreter so that they could question Edward Vieira as he recuperated from his operation to remove bullets from his hip and shoulder.

"The motive for this attack remains a mystery," police lieutenant Harvie Eubank told reporters. Referring to the brothers' limited vocal skills and communication difficulties, he said: "It is unlikely that they understood what was being said or what was happening. It was just a senseless shooting."

Another police officer, Detective Mitch Robins, told reporters: "They didn't understand what was going on. The car started pushing them against the curb and they went into a parking lot to stop and find out what was going on. The carload got out yelling and screaming at them. Maybe they were too close or the motorcycle was too noisy."

Eubank released composite drawings of two of the teenage suspects thought to be involved in the attack.

Police released these composites of two of the teen-age suspects being sought in the attack on two deaf brothers in Granada Hills on Sunday night.

2 Deaf Brothers Attacked; 1 Is Slain, the Other Wounded

Composite drawings issued by police to newspapers
Chicago Tribune

The sign language interpreter who assisted police in questioning Edward Vieira also accompanied police officers to the brothers' Palmdale home where they broke the sad news to Delores Vieira of her husband's death. She collapsed, utterly distraught, and her sister-in-law immediately rang Berenace Cree's house in Reseda using the TTY (deaf textphone). The mother and brother came over immediately to give comfort to the family and to help to deal with the police and reporters.

"I know my sons," Mrs. Cree told reporters. "They never hurt anyone."

"They never started trouble," their brother Marco added. "They would always mind their own business. They were innocent victims. It's like their handicap got them shot. People didn't understand them so they shot them."

"Just what happened is not fully clear. Obviously there were communication difficulties," Detective Robins told reporters. "But we strongly believe that, seeing as Cesar died and his wife is pregnant expecting a baby any day, one of the people in the vehicle should come forward and tell us what happened."

The next day, two of the teenagers heeded the call and came forward and told police that they were in the carload of teenagers involved in the confrontation that led to the shooting of the Vieira brothers. They identified a 16-year-old Long Beach boy as the shooter.

Police described the suspect as a member of a skinhead gang based in West Los Angeles. The two teenagers (a boy and a girl) who had come forward, with their parents, were not gang members but had just happened to be in the car getting a lift back from a Super Bowl party. They were upset, police said, that the victims were deaf and might not have understood what was happening. They were not expected to be charged, but police were concerned their version of the events differed from Edward Vieira's account.

In their version, the suspect had given the Vieira brothers a peace sign whilst they were halted at a traffic light, and one of the brothers had responded with what looked like a finger salute and had spat at the car. The would-be gunman had spat back before the motorcycle moved off on the green light.

In his version, Edward Vieira had said the brothers had done nothing to provoke the attack. They had simply been signing to each other.

Boy, 16, Shot Deaf Brothers, Police Told

■ Crime: Two teen-agers say a Long Beach youth killed one and wounded the other when a dispute escalated.

By MICHAEL CONNELLY
TIMES STAFF WRITER

A 16-year-old Long Beach boy is being sought as the gunman who shot two deaf brothers, killing one and wounding the other, in a scuffle in Granada Hills that witnesses said escalated from a stare-down contest between strangers at a traffic light, Los Angeles police said Thursday.

a car containing five teen-agers, police said.

During the ensuing confrontation, the brothers—who had limited speaking skills and normally communicated through sign language—were apparently unable to understand what was happening, police said. One of the teen-agers then opened fire with a handgun.

Police described the suspected gunman as an associate of members of a Skinhead gang based in West Los Angeles. However, detectives said the shooting of the Latino brothers apparently was not racially motivated.

The suspect's name and other details of his background were not released because he is a juvenile.

their version of events differs from Edward Vieira's account, he said.

According to Eubank, the two teen-agers said the shooting incident began when the teen-agers in the car and the men on the motorcycle started staring at each other at a traffic light. "They said it started as a stare-down contest and then somebody spit at the others and then they spit back," Eubank said.

Police said it was unclear who spit first or, in fact, if any spitting occurred. Edward Vieira has told investigators he and his brother did nothing that would have brought on the attack.

After the car followed the mo-

Headline in *Chicago Tribune*

The next day, police named the boy being sought for the shooting as Joey Bellinger. Originally, they had not revealed his identity because he was a juvenile but they had now been forced to do this because when they went to his parents' house to arrest him, they found that the boy had disappeared and both parents were refusing to say where he was. They would not give him up to the police unless there was a guarantee he would be tried in a juvenile court instead of as an adult. Police had refused to give this guarantee.

"He is not Billy the Kid, not John Dillinger, the father said of his son, "He's just a friendly boy who acted in self-defence." The father attacked police for the way they were targeting his son for the shooting.

Unfortunately for the Vieira family, once the media found out that it was the Bellinger family that was involved in the shootings, the name Vieira almost disappeared from the news. It was from then onwards almost all about the Bellinger family. They were much more interesting.

Three years previously, Joey Bellinger's sister Michelle had been murdered at the age of 16. Her body was discovered stuffed into three plastic garbage bags on a hillside in the Silver Lake district of Los Angeles. Her hand, chest and ankles were bound with duct tape. She had been severely beaten, raped then suffocated.

The siblings' father, Joe Bellinger, Sr., aged 40, had stalked the police investigation of his daughter's murder. He became an amateur pathologist, studying things such as patterns of rigor mortis and tissue decay to understand better police and medical examiner's reports; he stalked the streets and hillsides of Silver Lake looking for a car that a witness said might be involved in the killing. His obsession with the murder attracted media attention and even continued after a 15-year-old boy was arrested and convicted of the murder-rape as he felt that police had not arrested or found everyone involved in the crime.

Now, with his son allegedly involved in a different crime, he strove to portray him as a friendly boy with a few problems who had acted in fear of his life and therefore in self-defence when he shot the Vieira brothers. He went on a five-day hunger strike to draw attention to what he felt was police persecution of his family, arranged television interviews where he paraded two of the teenagers who were in the car and persuaded them to say that it was the Vieira brothers who caused the confrontation and got what they deserved. In another arranged television interview, he paraded a 15-year-old boy who he said was in the car and could understand American Sign Language and that the Vieira brothers were belligerent and made no attempt to communicate before the shooting.

The police responded to those allegations, saying that they had interviewed the youths in the car but "no one understands American Sign Language. The father is just trying to cover up his son's trail, that's all."

The elder Bellinger told the media that he was in contact with the boy but he would not co-operate with the police or turn him over until a promise was received that he would be tried as a juvenile. "This is my son's life," he said. "I'm doing everything I can to see that the truth is brought out".

"They want to crucify an innocent boy, who only fired in self defence and in fear of his life," Bellinger told a reporter. "They want me to supply the nails and the cross." Joey. Bellinger said, had told him that his hands were trembly, shaky and he just fired wildly.

In an attempt to discover the whereabouts of the fugitive, undercover police agents were following the father who was spotted in several payphone booths feeding quarters into the phone every three minutes, fuelling a belief by police that Joey Bellinger was in hiding out of California. One undercover police officer overheard the father discussing details of a police meeting he had just been to, and records showed that this call had been made long-distance to New York State.

Several other payphone records obtained by police also showed that these calls had been made to various payphones in upstate New York.

Interest in the Bellinger family was not confined to the police. Newspapers were ferreting around too, and reporters began questioning former neighbours in the Fairfax district where the family had lived at the time of the daughter's murder and found a different picture being painted of Joey Bellinger.

Many were not surprised that he had been the gunman in the shooting. One neighbour, who refused to be named, said that Joey Bellinger was "a walking time bomb, a kid who was waiting to kill or be killed."

Others said that he was a "spoilt, rich brat" who had been allowed to drop out of school after his sister's murder when only aged 14 with his father's indulgence.

He was alleged to be the leader of a gang called KAOS, which was said to be an acronym for 'Kids Against Our Society'. Residents said that they lived in fear of Joey Bellinger and his friends, who were not averse to terrorising the neighbourhood with a reign of fear or threats. Up to 15 youths would sometimes congregate at the Bellinger home and cause mayhem among the neighbourhood.

Most agreed that Joey Bellinger had gone off the rails following his sister's murder. "Everybody knew it was coming," said one. "People have felt for along time that Joey was an accident waiting to happen."

The previous year, there had been two attacks on the family home in Fairfax. One was a drive-by shooting which saw a bullet go through the plate glass window in the front lounge, and the other was a petrol bombing that had scorched the lawn.

After these two attacks, the neighbours had enough and petitioned the landlord to evict the Bellingers from the house they rented. The suit was filed in Los Angeles Municipal Court in September 1989 but in an out of court settlement, the Bellingers agreed to leave Fairfax and relocate to Long Beach.

A police spokesman agreed that there had been gang-related problems linked with Joey Bellinger but dismissed KAOS as a "wannabe gang of white youths who probably used narcotics and believed in racial segregation." They were primarily known, he said, for defacing the Fairfax district with graffiti.

This, then, was Joey Bellinger being painted in a different picture from that of his father who proclaimed him an innocent, friendly boy in fear of his life.

By the end of February, police had a good idea where Joey Bellinger was. The family had originally come to California from New York State and they discovered that Joey's mother, Phyllis, still had friends in upstate New York where she had attended school. They traced Joey to a house in Cassville, New York State, owned by an old school friend of Phyllis named Susan Alguire who had been contacted by Joey's mother on 30 January asking if she could put up Joey for a temporary period until the family managed to relocate back to New York. The friend had been completely unaware that Joey Bellinger was a fugitive wanted for murder.

He was arrested by FBI agents on 2 March and was arraigned before Oneida County Court on 6 March where he consented to return to California without an extradition hearing.

The following week, his mother Phyllis Mary Goodman and his father, Joseph Paul Bellinger were also arrested and charged with aiding and abetting a felon. They were freed on bail and ordered to return to court on 18 April for a preliminary hearing. In the meantime, Joey Bellinger was returned to California and charged with the murder of Cesar Vieira and attempted murder of Edward Vieira and remanded in custody pending a hearing to determine if he would be prosecuted as an adult or as a juvenile.

The parents appeared in Long Beach Municipal Court on 26 June and pleaded guilty to the charges of aiding and abetting a suspected felon. They admitted they had helped their son to flee Southern California to Upstate New York to avoid prosecution for the shooting of the two deaf brothers.

Under the terms of a plea agreement reached with the parents' defence attorneys, Joseph Paul Bellinger was sentenced to 30 days in the County Jail and probation for three years. Phyllis Mary Goodman was sentenced to the same length of probation, but with no jail time.

It was to be another two years before Joey Bellinger would face trial to answer the charges of murder and attempted murder levied against him. Much of these two years were devoted to hearings to decide if he would stand trial as an adult and to psychiatric hearings.

When Joey Bellinger finally appeared in San Fernando Superior Court before Judge Howard J. Schwab on 27 October 1992, his Defence Attorney Ezekiel P. Perlo, had successfully negotiated a plea bargain with the District Attorney's office that allowed him to plead guilty to voluntary manslaughter.

The court heard that Bellinger had been in a car with four other young people when they drew up at a traffic light beside the motorcycle being driven by the Vieira brothers, who were conversing with each other in sign language.

Bellinger, a member of a Westside gang called KAOS, flashed a gang sign – a "K" for KAOS, and one of the brothers allegedly responded by raising his middle finger. This led to a confrontation a few minutes later in a shopping centre car park, where Joey Bellinger produced a gun and shot dead one of the brothers, seriously wounding another.

Deputy District Attorney Phil Halpin told the court that his officer had agreed to the plea bargain settlement because some witnesses had disappeared, making it more difficult to obtain a conviction if the case went to trial. If Bellinger had not accepted a plea bargain, he could have been sentenced to life in prison if found guilty.

"This is a tragic case. There are no winners, only losers," Judge Schwab told the court as he sentenced Bellinger to twelve years in prison, with credit for the nearly three years he had already been in custody and more than a year for good behaviour. This meant that he would be eligible for parole in four years time after serving seven years.

As part of the plea bargain, it was agreed that Bellinger would serve his time in a California Youth Authority facility.

Chapter 7

1991: Milwaukee, USA

Murdered and Dismembered

It was only a matter of time before a Deaf person became one of the victims of a serial killer. This fate befell Tony Hughes in Milwaukee in May 1991.

Deaf since early childhood, Tony was educated at the Wisconsin State School for the Deaf in Delavan, approximately 50 miles from Milwaukee. An intelligent, friendly and popular man who communicated effectively through lipreading, gesture and writing with his hearing friends but his preferred means of communication was American Sign Language. He had a wide circle of Deaf friends and was also well known in Milwaukee's gay community where he frequented the many bars that gay people met in.

He was 31 years old when he dropped out from sight and people began to be concerned as at first weeks, then months went by without any word or sight from him. The Deaf community is quite small, and people will soon begin to notice if someone has not been around for sometime.

It was not just the Deaf community. The gay community in Milwaukee was just as concerned. Perhaps they had more cause. For some time, there had been unexplained disappearances of gay men within the city and Tony Hughes' disappearance only served to fuel the unease that was being felt.

No one, however, was prepared for the shocking findings that began to emerge in late July 1991 when police raided an apartment complex in one of the seedier districts of Milwaukee. It was an area of boarded up shops, sleazy homosexual bars, strip joints, frequented by muggers and mini-skirted hookers and most of those who lived there rented cheap one-room apartments from under $300 a month.

The police had originally been called to the apartment by a black man who had handcuffs dangling from his left wrist who had accosted a patrol car crew and given them a hysterical tale about someone who was trying to kill him. In order to pacify him, the police officers agreed to accompany him to a whiter two-storey building called Oxford Apartments, a government subsidised rooming house occupied almost exclusively by black people.

Tony Hughes

The police officers had already been told that the would-be killer lived in Room 213, and gained entrance into the building by ringing a different apartment bell and telling the occupants that they were police and wanted to enter the building. The black man went in with them.

The tall, good-looking young white male who answered the door answered their questions politely, looking at his accuser as if he had never seen them before. When the police asked the occupant for the key to the handcuffs, he tried to stall. When they insisted, he refused and his calm vanished. He suddenly went berserk and there was a brief, violent struggle as the occupant and the two police officers wrestled in the doorway of the apartment, the noise attracting other residents who heard one of the officers yell: "The son of a bitch has bitten me!"

Finally however, the officers had the man face down on the floor, handcuffed, with his rights being dictated to him. They also became aware of an unpleasant odour of decay not unlike rotten fish that pervaded the whole of the apartment. Police were later to find out that other residents had regularly complained about the smell.

A radio call to headquarters to run a check on the suspect soon brought forth an answer that the man had previously been convicted for sexual assault and for enticing a 13-year-old boy. This gave the police justification to inspect the foul-smelling apartment.

"Oh my God! There's a goddamn head in here!"

One of the officers was retching near an upright refrigerator and quickly clearing the apartment, the police officers radioed for assistance and the presence of a scene-of-crimes unit to go over the apartment thoroughly.

Milwaukee police carrying body bags out of the apartment for forensic tests.

Soon, the apartment was swarming with forensic investigators and the suspect was transported, still handcuffed and resisting violently, to the local precinct where he admitted his name was Jeffrey Dahmer.

The forensic investigators found in their search of the apartment that it was a mixture of torture chamber and slaughterhouse. The nauseous finds included plastic bags in the freezer compartment of the refrigerator that looks suspiciously like human flesh, one of which looked like a human heart. Another freezer contained three plastic bags, each with a human head and a filing cabinet contained five more skulls, which had been painted grey plus other body parts. Two more skulls were found in a pan while another contained severed human hands and a cut-off penis.

Several of the skulls were created for the purpose of being used as sex toys. There had been holes drilled in them, through which caustic liquids had been dribbled in an effort to destroy the subject's conscious will. Needless to say, this weird approach to neurosurgery had a 100 percent failure rate and none of the victims survived.

There was a stinking blue plastic barrel that contained three human torsos and an electric saw stained with blood that made it clear how Dahmer had dismembered his victims.

In all, 11 heads and skulls were found in the apartment, along with numerous pieces of other body parts including hands, internal organs, muscle pieces, penises. Some of the body parts had clearly been cooked and eaten. Police discovered that Dahmer had little food in the apartment except potato crisps, human meat and a jar of mustard.

In his bedroom, Dahmer had built a macabre makeshift altar, decorated with candles and human skulls.

Jeffrey Dahmer

Tony Hughes' skull was one of those identified in the apartment, apparently forming part of Dahmer's skull trophy collection.

In all, police accredited Dahmer with the murders of 17 young men, most of whom were gay. The earliest attributed to him occurred in 1978 in Ohio when Dahmer was only 18 years old, just before he enlisted in the US Army and was sent to Germany. There was a gap of 9 years before the second murder took place in 1987 although some uncertainty existed as to whether the unsolved murder of a German girl named Ericka Handschuh in 1980 could be attributed to Dahmer. This took place in Baumholder, West Germany where Dahmer was based as a medic.

From 1987 to 1989, Dahmer killed four people before his murderous activities were brought to a halt by his conviction for enticing a 13-year-old Laotian boy to his apartment for sexual reasons.

Despite requests by the prosecution for a custodial sentence of five to six years, the judge only sentenced Dahmer to a one-year prison term and five years probation, bowing to defence reasoning that psychological counselling would be of greater benefit than a long custodial sentence.

When Dahmer came out of prison after serving 10 months in May 1990, he had changed. He vowed he would not make the same mistake again as he had with the young boy – there would be more no survivors. He was also no longer content simply to strangle his victims as he had done before his conviction. He now wanted to eat them, and have sex with their dead bodies before he dismembered them. He also wanted to collect souvenirs of his victims, hence his skull collection, some of which he bleached and painted grey. He also collected the penises of his victims, but was stumped how to preserve this collection in a good state.

Asked in his only television interview why he did this, he said: "I killed not because I was angry with them, not because I hated them, but because I wanted to keep them or parts of them with me."

In the space of 12 months since moving into room 213 in Oxford Apartments in June 1990, Dahmer killed 12 young men, and the gaps between each killing were becoming smaller, his final attempt that led to his arrest coming only three days after he had murdered his 17th victim.

The majority of Dahmer's victims were unknown to him. He picked them up casually in one of the many gay bars in Milwaukee, a favourite being the gay Club 219, and invite them back to his apartment for sex. Once he had the prospective victim inside the apartment, Dahmer would drug him then manacle him to a chair or one of the pipes in the apartment so that he could amuse himself with his victim at his leisure in relative safety.

Tony Hughes was a little different from all Dahmer's other victims. They had met at a party in early 1990, and they had since then bumped into each other several times in various gay bars, becoming "friends", communicating by handwritten notes and through Hughes lipreading Dahmer.

However, on 24 May 1991, the Deaf gay man made the fatal mistake of accepting a written proposition from Dahmer to go to his apartment to pose for photographs for $50 and to have sex. This was a ruse that Dahmer had used several times, but this was the only time he actually wrote his request down.

Tony Hughes' family at a memorial service for Dahmer's victims

Jeffrey Dahmer in court

Once Jeffrey Dahmer got Tony Hughes into his apartment, he had him drugged like all the others then killed and dismembered, his skull being added to the skull collection. Tony Hughes was Jeffrey Dahmer's thirteenth victim.

There were four more victims in quick succession before Dahmer was arrested on 22 July.

By August 1991, Dahmer had been charged with 15 counts of murder in Wisconsin and on 30 January 1992, Dahmer went on trial before Judge Lawrence Cram. On the advice of his defence team, he filed a plea of guilty but insane to all 15 murders. The trial then became a battle between prosecution and defence psychologists. After two weeks, on 15 February 1992, the jury took only five hours to reject the plea of guilty but insane, returning a verdict that found Dahmer sane and responsible for his actions.

Judge Cram structured all the 15 life sentences in such a way that Dahmer would have to theoretically serve a minimum total of 936 years, therefore ensuring he would never be released.

Jeffrey Dahmer still faced being indicted with the two murders he committed in his grandmother's house in Ohio. Although prosecutors in Ohio subsequently charged him with one of the murders, he was never brought to trial. As Ohio still had the death penalty, he could not be extradited from Wisconsin without a legal hearing and prosecutors in Ohio felt that there was no point in seeking extradition and going to the expense of a major trial when it was clear Dahmer would never be released from Wisconsin's prison system.

In prison, Dahmer refused offers of protective custody despite many threats against his life by other prisoners. Dahmer emerged unscathed with a few minor scratches from one attempt by a prisoner to cut his throat while they were in the prison chapel. He refused to press charges against that prisoner, but a few months later, on 28 November 1994, Dahmer was part of a prison work detail cleaning a bathroom next to the gym in the Columbia Correctional Institute, Portage, Wisconsin, when another member of the work detail, 25-year-old Christopher Scarver, grabbed an iron bar from a nearby exercise machine and brought it down on Dahmer's skull, smashing it and killing him instantly.

Chapter 8

1992: Los Angeles, USA

Wrongly Interpreted

Gang-related violence does not usually touch upon the lives of people involved in the Deaf Community unless, as with the Epkins and Vieira cases, these Deaf people fall innocent victim to hearing gang members they have no involvement with. This case is an exception because members of two Deaf gangs were involved and it could not happen anywhere else in the world except in Los Angeles.

The Van Nuys apartment building block at 15300 Vanowen Street housed a number of Deaf residents who would naturally receive from time to time Deaf friends as visitors. Friday 10 January 1992 was no different from any other night when friends of Deaf residents dropped into various apartments.

James E. Powell Jr., a 27-year-old Deaf Black from Long Beach used the occasion to visit his girlfriend, Yvonne Burnita, for an evening of congenial pleasure. Powell was known to the police to have connections with local gangs and it was unfortunate for him that three rival gang members spotted him going into Burnita's apartment.

Howard Love aged 26, and Val Lamar Smith, aged 21, plus one other unnamed man, who all came from South-Central Los Angeles were also Deaf with severe speech impediments. They also happened to be visiting friends in the same apartment block on the same night. They had an ongoing gang-related dispute with James E. Powell, so when they spotted him going into Burnita's apartment, they decided to resolve their dispute with him and confronted Powell in the young woman's apartment.

During the fight that ensued, Smith produced a gun and shot Powell several times. As Powell fell dying, the two men fled the scene whilst neighbours in other apartments, disturbed by the confrontation called police.

When police questioned Yvonne Burnita she denied that she had witnessed the shooting, insisting she was having a nap at the time in another bedroom and did not hear the gunshots. However, she later admitted she had lied because she was scared the members of the other gang would seek revenge upon her. When she was questioned for a second time, she gave the police the names of those who had invaded her apartment and shot her boyfriend and it did not take the police long to trace the two men.

It was only when Smith and Love were arrested and taken to Van Nuys police precinct for questioning that an issue arose which was to cause numerous pre-trial motions and hearings over the next few years. The point at issue was whether Val Lamar Smith received proper sign language interpretation during the police interrogations.

The arrest and subsequent pre-trial hearings also highlighted two different forms of American Sign Language, one the more formal version that has its roots in the "white" deaf sub-culture, the other a less stylised form of sign language that has its roots in the segregated American South and lives on today in poor, predominantly African American neighbourhoods where access to special schools, plus training and social opportunities for Deaf African Americans is often limited. The informal, stylised ASL found among this group of Deaf people is very different from the more accepted form of ASL generally in use and not many people outside this social sub-group, deaf or hearing, could understand its use.

The sign language interpreter provided by the police for Smith and Love was not familiar with this style of informal ASL that Smith and Love used.

While this was academic in the case of Howard Love who accepted a plea bargain to plead guilty to a charge of voluntary manslaughter in exchange for a three-year prison term and a promise to testify against Smith, the use of a sign language interpreter who was not familiar with Smith's style of communication raised questions at a later stage over the accuracy of the translations. In particular, whether Smith's lack of proficiency in formal ASL led to him being denied his Miranda rights to remain silent or have an attorney present when questioned by police. There were also questions that focused on whether what Smith said to the interviewing officers was properly translated by the police sign language interpreter.

When asked by police whether he wished give up his right to remain silent, the interpreter translated Smith's response as saying he did not want to talk and "I prefer to go to court and I want a lawyer." Taking that to mean Smith wanted a lawyer only in court and not during the interrogation, police proceeded to question him.

Whereas the defence attorney contented that Smith's statements made during his interrogation should not be admitted into evidence as he had not waived his right to remain silent and police had ignored his request for an attorney to be present, Deputy District Attorney Shellie Samuels, for Van Nuys County, said that Smith had created the ambiguity himself by not clearly saying what he wanted and the fact the police videotaped the interrogation proved that no misconduct took place, or was intended.

The trial of Val Lamar Smith was fixed for January 1994. It would be what the prosecution called a "very straightforward murder case". It would be true to say it was depressingly similar to hundreds of other killings that happen in Los Angeles. Young men, allegedly members of different gangs, bump into each other and somebody is left for dead. But the Val Lamar Smith case was unique. Almost all the principal characters - the defendant, the victim, the witnesses – were all Deaf. Even the trial judge, Superior Court Judge Michael Farrell, described himself as hearing-impaired with less than 50% hearing in both ears in the conversational range, the result of Army service as a tank crew member.

The trial would also have to bridge the gap between the two different forms of American Sign Language – that mainly used by the majority of "white" and educated Deaf Blacks, and the stylised dialect used by poor African American Deaf people.

Using two different sets of ASL interpreters would do this. In Los Angeles, it was said that after Spanish, sign language interpreting was the second most frequently translated language in the court system and the Los Angeles County Courts interpreter services employed 10 American Sign Language interpreters. Karen Bowman, who would be the principal interpreter used to bridge the gap between the two forms of ASL, was one of them. She was herself Deaf.

However, before the trial could actually take place, the court had to sit through two weeks of pre-trial motions during which Smith's attorney, Tony Bryan, pressed for the exclusion from evidence of all statements made by Smith in Van Nuys police station, arguing that his Miranda rights had been violated.

Judge Michael Farrell told the prosecution and defence attorneys that he found there was great ambiguity in the translation of what Smith had said in the police station under interrogation. He thought it was fortunate that the interrogation had been videotaped, and this had enabled the court to see that Smith had not waived his rights and had wanted a lawyer at the time of the interrogation.

"He (the defendant) did not waive his rights at the beginning of the interview," Judge Farrell told the court. "He did ask for a lawyer." However, he made a tentative ruling allowing Smith's statement to be used.

"The purpose of suppression (of evidence) is to punish police who may have forced a confession. As we have seen in the videotapes, this is clearly not the case here. The police did everything to make it fair but the interrogating officer was honestly confused by what Smith had said," he told the court. "Police had not understood at what point he wanted an attorney."

To support his ruling, Judge Farrell said that the investigators had acted in good faith because their ASL interpreter had created an ambiguity when she told detectives Smith had said, "I prefer to go to court and I want a lawyer."

In addition to making this ruling, Judge Farrell also ruled that the jury could hear an incriminating statement that Smith made to the police. In this statement, Smith admitted that he had fired two shots into Powell's body and leg but denied having fired the fatal shot into the victim's head.

Val Lamar Smith in court
Los Angeles Times photo by Joel P. Lugavere

Having lost the pre-trial arguments to keep the videotaped statement from being used in evidence, Val Lamar Smith was advised by his attorney to waive his right to a trial and allow the judge to decide his fate. This was because it was clear that he would most certainly be convicted in a seldom-used procedure technically called a "submission on transcript" but most commonly known as a "slow plea".

In the rarely-used "slow plea" procedure, a defendant maintains certain constitutional rights including avoiding having to plead guilty. These rights include the right to appeal the judge's decision, which is taken after consideration of various documents.

The decision also saved Los Angeles County Court authorities the expense of a difficult, possibly long-drawn out trial involving the use of numerous sign language interpreters.

After reviewing police transcripts and other documents, and having the police interview videotapes translated for him, Judge Farrell sentenced Smith to a prison term of 15 years to life, and urged him to take advantage of any educational opportunities he might be offered in prison.

"The defendant admits nothing," his defence attorney Tony Bryan told reporters. "It was understood the court was probably going to convict and we have saved what could have been along and expensive trial. We will appeal at the earliest possible opportunity."

Judge Farrell conceded that an appeal court may disagree with his decision. If his decision involving

Smith's constitutional rights is overturned by the Court of Appeal, his conviction would also be overturned. If the case is sent back to Farrell's court, Deputy District Attorney Samuels, for the State, told the defendant that he would be prosecuted for first-degree murder, a crime that carries a penalty of 25 years to life in prison.

Chapter 9

1994: England

The Motorway Murders

The 1990s England saw a continued increase in road traffic throughout the country with more and more roads and motorways being built or upgraded. Due to the decline of rail freight services, much of this increase in road traffic was in lorries or other haulage vehicles.

Accompanying this increase in road freight services was an increase in young women frequenting motorway service stations. Some of these women were students, particularly from Europe, who were trying to save money by hitching lifts. However, there were other young women frequenting these places who were prostitutes and whose sole purpose for being there was to ply their trade. For these women, long-distance lorry drivers and other commercial travellers were sought-after customers.

However, the reverse was also true. The very customers that these prostitutes targeted had within their ranks some predatory rapists and woman-abusers. The transitional nature of their occupations meant that they could move quickly from one place to another along British motorways making it difficult for their victims or the police to trace them.

It was not long before some of these abuses turned to murder and several police forces in various parts of the country found themselves investigating dead bodies of women who had casually been abandoned by the road verges, ditches or fields adjoining roads. Most of these bodies turned up around the English Midland counties where there was an intensive network of motorways.

The first of these killings was of Janine Downes whose body was found in a lay-by on the A464 between Telford and Wolverhampton near the M54 motorway in 1991 then Natalie Pearman, aged only 16 but a known drug addict and prostitute, was found just outside Norwich on the A11 in November 1992. Another prostitute, Carol Clark aged 32, was found dumped at the docks at Sharpness, Gloucester, near the M5 after leaving a note for her boyfriend in March 1993 telling him she was going to look for a client at Gordano service station, Bristol.

Then Samo Paull, a 20 year-old Birmingham prostitute vanished in December 1993 and was later found strangled in a water-filled ditch near the village of Swinford, Leicestershire.

When Tracy Turner, a partially-deaf prostitute who had a habit of picking up lorry drivers at motorway service stations was also found dumped on the grass verge of a quiet country lane in Bittleswell, near Lutterworth, Leicestershire, on 4 March 1994 only two miles from where Samo Paull's body had been found, police started to believe that they had a serial killer on the loose who were picking up prostitutes from motorway areas.

What particularly interested detectives (and the national press who were quick to put two and two together) was that both Samo Paull and Tracy Turner, whose body had been found completely naked except for a hearing aid cord around her neck that had been used to strangle her, were found only a few miles from the M1/M6 motorway junction. Both women had been engaged in sex before being strangled. In Tracy Turner's case, the sex had been unprotected and had been, in the words of the police, particularly enthusiastic.

Although police feared a serial killer on the loose, they were careful not to allow their fears to be made public and, still, the killings continued with a 19-year old Sheffield prostitute, Dawn Shields, being found by the roadside near Mam Tor in the Derbyshire Peak District in May 1994.

In August 1994, June Finley, 23, a prostitute from the Liverpool area, was found dumped half-naked in a field off the A570 in Skelmersdale, Lancashire. The spot where she was found was only a couple of miles from the M58, which led from Liverpool to the M6.

In the perception of the British public, the murder of a prostitute is an unremarkable thing and is accepted as one of the risks that women who take up the sex trade run. Therefore the series of killings were not prominently reported in the national press. However, things changed when a French student vanished after being seen getting into the cab of a white Mercedes lorry at Chieveley service station on the M4 on 19 December 1995.

Celine Figard, an 18-year-old student, had hitchhiked from France to spend the Christmas holidays with a relative living in the New Forest area of England. She never arrived and her disappearance was featured prominently in the national press, with appeals on television for her whereabouts to be made known.

Her body was found in a lay-by just off the M5 near Worcester 10 days later on 29 December. A post mortem determined that her body had been kept refrigerated for a length of time, probably since after she was shortly killed, and had only just been dumped. Police strongly suspected a refrigerated trailer had been used for the storage of the body over the Christmas period. The body showed signs of sexual assault and like the bodies of the prostitutes, she had been strangled and was naked.

Celine's murder was the first time that the police admitted they were looking at the possibility there was a lorry driver serial killer on the loose and the national media brought back to public attention the killings of Samo Paull and Tracy Turner in particular to focus attention on rogue lorry drivers. The police, however, were quick to deny they had specifically linked all the killings.

As a result of police enquiries, haulage companies started checking journeys taken by their drivers. One firm, Christian Salvesen, that had a depot close to where the body of the French student had been found said: "We will assist the police in any way possible and we have begun to track the movements of drivers over the past fortnight by checking our records."

Through the co-operation of haulage firms, it was only a matter of time before police were able to zero in on one particular suspect who had boasted to other drivers that he had sex regularly with hitchhikers. The suspect also had a wife and a mistress at opposite ends of the country who were unknown to each other.

Stuart Morgan lived with his second wife in Poole, Dorset and kept a mistress in Wigan, Lancashire, only a few miles from Skelmersdale where Julie Finley's body was found. Both wife and mistress thought that they shared their lives alone with their lorry driver partner and accepted his lengthy absences as being due to the nature of his job as a freelance driver for a Southampton firm that took him all over the country as well as Europe.

Although he was linked (but not charged) with the murder of Julie Finley, there was irrefutable evidence linking him to the murder of Celine Figard and Morgan was sentenced for life at Winchester Crown Court in October 1996 for her murder.

To the dismay of police, however, Morgan's DNA did not match samples taken from Tracy Turner and they realised they were looking for a <u>SECOND</u> lorry driver killer.

However, the intense search for lorry driver travel records by police and haulage companies had unearthed another possibility who was linked with a rape in Exeter. Arrested for this rape, Alun Kyte, a 32-year-old man from Stafford was sentenced to seven years imprisonment.

What excited the police most was that his DNA matched the samples taken from Tracy Turner and they arranged for Kyte to be transferred to a prison near Leicester to facilitate questioning.

Tracy Turner
Her body was found naked, except for a hearing aid
cord pulled tightly round her neck

Whilst in the Leicester prison, Kyte bragged to other prisoners that he had attacked at least 12 women including Tracy Turner.

Alun Kyte

He was alleged to have said that: "She laughed as they had sex and I kept strangling her until she stopped."

However, this boast and the DNA samples alone were insufficient evidence to allow the police to charge Kyte with Tracy Turner's murder and they desperately needed other evidence.

This came from a keen-eyed car passenger named Betty Wilson who was with her husband when she spotted a car being driven by Kyte with a woman propped up in the back seat.

"Her face was black and blue in patches. I realised she was dead because I used to work in a hospital," she was to tell the court almost seven years later.

A few days later, she read an appeal in the *News of the World* for information about Samo Paull and instantly recognised the woman in the appeal picture as the one she had seen propped up in the car back seat.

Although she reported her sighting to the police, she had unfortunately not been able to describe the make of the car or its registration number therefore it was another four years following his conviction for the Exeter rape that police were able to link this crucial evidence to Alun Kyte. Together with the DNA evidence from Tracy Turner's murder and Kyte's boasts to other prisoners in Leicester about what he had done to his victims, this was enough to convict him when he finally appeared at Nottingham Crown Court in March 2000 charged with the murders of Samo Paull and Tracy Turner, killings which the police had always believed were linked.

Alun Kyte was given two life sentences for these murders on top of the seven he was already serving for the Exeter rape.

However, police believed that Kyte was responsible for the murders of at least twelve other prostitutes and were keen to question him in order to put all the other cases to rest.

Note: The story of the murder of Tracy Turner was originally written by the author in Deaf Crime Casebook, published in 1997, before Alun Kyte was arrested.

Chapter 10

1995: Moscow, Russia

Executed by the Mafia

In the old Communist Russia, the lot of Deaf people was a very miserable one. A sizeable proportion of deaf people under the age of 40 were the unlucky products of a health system that was not too fussy about prescribing too many antibiotics hailed as a cure for all ills in the late 1950s and early 1960s. The risks of side effects were conveniently and routinely ignored. As a result, it was estimated that up to 90% of the membership of the Moscow Association for the Deaf in 1990 were victims of badly prescribed antibiotics.

Regimented like many of the hearing Soviet Union's citizens, deaf people were educated wherever schools for the deaf were established and when they finished their education, the State allocated them jobs. If they wore hearing aids, they were only able to use bulky Soviet-made aids that were liable to breakdown. Adapted telephones and any other technological gadgets that the West had now come to take for granted were unaffordable to the majority of Soviet Russia's citizens. On the plus side, many Deaf people could survive and go about their lives with some measure of relative safety.

When Russia threw off the Communist yoke, many Deaf people found themselves fighting for survival. Unlike the old Soviet regime where jobs were guaranteed, they found that post-Soviet Russia no longer even guaranteed them work. As a result, many

Deaf people suddenly found it hard to survive and growing numbers started to turn to crime in the rough, tough new Russia. Commonly this involved drugs and prostitution. As Vladimir Bazenov, the deputy head of the Moscow Association for the Deaf was to say, "Drugs dealing is an increasing attractive option for many deaf people."

A young Deaf woman named Svetlana, aged 17, was a prime example. Spotted in Moscow's Pushkin Square by a Western journalist, she told him through a sign language interpreter that she was one of about 50 deaf drug pushers operating in Moscow dealing with anything from heroin to hashish. The pushers were controlled by a single deaf mafia, headed by 5 bosses. Earning about £70 for an evening's work, she told the journalist that she had been recruited into the gang by foul means, by one of the five bosses threatening to kill her if she did not pay him protection money. She had already served a short prison term for drugs dealing and the journalist found scores of deaf people signing outside Moscow's railway stations, hotels and street corners trying to sell drugs. They tended to be ignored by the police who were perhaps themselves receiving bribes from crime bosses to look the other way.

To try and encourage disabled people to work, the new Russia allowed companies whose workforce comprised of over 70% disabled people to claim exemption from various taxes, including VAT and customs duties on imports and exports. Unfortunately, such companies became very attractive to unscrupulous non-disabled businessmen looking for ways to avoid taxes. Many of these businessmen were also part of the growing Russian mafia who were looking for ways and means of laundering money obtained through illegal activities, including drugs. A manager of any company employing disabled people who got involved with these tax scams was flirting with danger if they fell out with the demands of the mafia businessmen.

That's why nobody in Moscow was surprised when one such company manager was shot dead in the doorway of his apartment on 7 September 1995, although the murder itself sent shock waves through the international Deaf community.

Igor Abramov was born in the small village of Kursk, south of Moscow, and became deaf when aged 13. Following this, he attended the Moscow School for the Deaf from which he graduated with high grades. He then attended the Moscow State University of Technology from which he received a master's degree in optical electronics in 1981.

He then began working as a researcher for the Soviet military industry. His undoubted talent saw him elected President of the Moscow Society for the Deaf in 1985. He also served as a vice president of the All-Russian Federation of the Deaf from 1990 to 1992. Both these positions gave him the opportunity to travel extensively and participate in a number of international conferences for the deaf, especially in America. At the first International Conference on Deaf History at Gallaudet University, he presented a paper and shared with the author his experiences of post-Soviet Russia.

These travels, coupled with periods of study at Gallaudet University, the National Technical Institute for the Deaf at Rochester, New York, and at the California State University gave him a desire to bring to Deaf Russians a post-secondary educational programme. To achieve this, he earned a doctorate in education from the Russian Academy of Science before becoming the deputy director in charge of special deaf programmes at the Educational Centre at Moscow State University of Technology.

Abramov was presented with the Edward Miner Gallaudet Award of the Laurent Clerc Cultural Fund of the Gallaudet University Alumni Association in April 1994 for his services to Deaf Russians. At the time of his assassination, he had been selected to be the Powrie Vaux Doctor Chair of Deaf Studies at Gallaudet University for the 1996-1997 academic year.

Igor Abramov's downfall was due to his status as manager of two companies that employed over 70% disabled people in their workforce, thus qualifying for exemption from various taxes. This made him a juicy target for unscrupulous businessmen and in exchange for a cut of the profits, he allowed these businessmen to use his companies' rubber stamps and signature as a cover for their own operations. By July 1995, Igor Abramov was enjoying the trappings of wealth. He was not afraid of showing his pack of credit cards and also showed off his purchase of a brand new Cherokee Jeep which had cost him over £35,000.

Several of his friends and colleagues in the Moscow Society for the Deaf were concerned and worried about the direction Igor Abramov was taking and tried to warn him not to get in too deep.

But it was too late. Igor Abramov had fallen out with one of the businessmen whose operations he was rubber-stamping.

On the evening of 7 September 1995, Igor Abramov answered the ringing of the doorbell in his apartment in Moscow and upon opening it, was confronted with a masked gunman. Turning to flee, he was shot in the back of his head. Another shot to the back of the head was made after he had fallen facedown in a pool of blood.

The police investigation, which linked the assassination to Abramov's "entrepreneurial activities" got nowhere.

Igor Abramov was not the first, or last, prominent Deaf Russian to fall foul of the Mafia.

Vycheslav Skomorokhov, a famed Russian athlete, was shot dead in a bar in 1992 aged 52. In his heyday, he represented Russia in the World Games for the Deaf in 1965, 1968 and 1973 winning gold medals in the 100m and 400m hurdles. Altogether, he won 8 gold medals in these games. He also represented Russia in the 1968 Olympics in Mexico City where he came 5th in the 400m hurdles final.

In 1998, Abramov's successor as the President of the All-Russian Society for the Deaf, Valery Korablinov, was also assassinated.

At the time of writing, all three assassinations are still unsolved. Deaf Russians are reluctant to talk about anything linked with these killing and an attempt by the author to find out more details met with a brick wall.

Vycheslav Skomorokhov (second from left) running in the final of the 400 metres hurdles final, in Mexico City 1968. He was fifth after John Sherwood (GBR), left, who was third, and David Hemery (GBR), far right, who won the gold.
He was the first prominent Deaf Russian to be assassinated by the Mafia in Moscow (1992).

Chapter 11

1998: Durban, South Africa

Murdered by Cops!

Everyone accepts that polices sometimes make mistakes just like everyone else. However, when police officers make mistakes that lead to the deaths of innocent people, questions need to be asked and action taken to prevent repetition.

The year 2000 was a particularly bad year for police mistakes in mid-West America, where two separate shootings by police officers resulted in the deaths of deaf people.

The first occurred in Tennessee on Thursday 24 February 2000 when two Wilkinson County Sheriff's Deputies went to a house in Bear Creek with a warrant for the arrest of a man on a domestic violence complaint. They knew the man they went to arrest, Bruce Gilbert, was Deaf as he had previously served a five-year prison sentence for sexual battery on a child under 13.

The complaint leading to the issue of the warrant had been filled out by Bruce Gilbert's mother who had alleged that her son had acted erratically, 'got up in her face', thrown the family dog across the room and had shaken a rifle shell at her, though he never actually hit or harmed her. The sole purpose of Martha Faye Raines, Gilbert's mother, in filing the complaint was to try and get psychiatric help for her son. She warned the officers her son might be dangerous to himself. She never imagined the tragic consequences to her son that would follow her complaint to the Sheriff's Office.

When Deputies Demerest and Durbin arrived at the Gilbert home at 3794 Bear Creek Road, they got out of the car and spotted Gilbert shovelling gravel out of a ditch. They walked up behind him, grabbed his arms and swung him round. According to the officers, they tried to show Gilbert a handwritten sign that told him he was under arrest but he hit one of them on the hand twice. This could be interpreted as trying to grab the handwritten note to read it better, but he was judged to be resisting arrest and sprayed with Mace, hit with a baton and slammed against the wall of his house in front of horrified relatives. He broke free from the officers and stumbled across to the ditch where he had been working and came tripped over his shovel.

Anguished relatives and neighbours after the shooting of Bruce Gilbert

As he stood up, he held his shovel out in front of him. According to the officers, he was swinging the shovel at them; according to eyewitnesses, he was just assuming a defensive position because he couldn't see due to the Mace and was stepping back. Whatever the version, this was the signal for both officers to open fire. Five bullets slammed into Gilbert's chest, lifting him off the ground and slamming him down on his back.

Shocked relatives howled, screamed and hurled abuse at the officers who called in to the Sheriff's Office and requested back up.

Bruce Gilbert was 35 years old, and had been educated at the Tennessee School for the Deaf, Knoxville where he excelled in sports. However, he never had a steady job and worked around the Bear Creek community doing odd jobs.

Relatives were severely critical of the conduct of the two officers and did not feel the shooting was justified.

"You just never approach a deaf person from behind the way these officers did," said an aunt.

Mary McKinney, executive director of the League for the Hearing Impaired, which offers deaf awareness training for law enforcement agencies, also criticised the police conduct.

"Deaf people have been shot before because they had their backs to the police and did not hear any request to stop."

Ms. McKinney also said that police had infringed Bruce Gilbert's rights. They had known he was Deaf in advance of executing the warrant, and should have waited for the arrival of a sign language interpreter before trying to arrest him.

Six months later, a similar incident- this time in Detroit – shocked America once again.

Police officers from Detroit's 8th (Northwest) Precinct were called to a house in Ferguson and

Nichols in response to a telephone call that mentioned a domestic disturbance was taking place.

When they arrived at 4 p.m. on Tuesday 28 August 2000, they saw a man holding a rake in the driveway of his home apparently making threatening motions with it.

Neighbours and relatives grasped the danger to the man immediately the officers drew their guns.

"Don't shoot! He's deaf!" the man's mother yelled at the officers.

"He's deaf, he's deaf, he's deaf!" a young woman later identified as his niece was screaming.

"He's mute, he's deaf, he can't hear!" a neighbour shouted.

All this was in vain. The police officers opened fire immediately, and the man fell with two shots in his side.

The man, Errol Shaw who was Deaf and could not speak, died that night of his wounds in the Sinai-Grace Hospital in Detroit.

As in the Tennessee case, police officers justified their actions as 'acting in self-defence' but neighbours and relatives severely criticised their conduct. They alleged that police officers and detectives stood around laughing and joking as they secured the scene, ignoring the shot man as he lay wounded on the driveway, and waited too long to call emergency services to take Shaw to hospital.

Neighbours described him as "Errol the yardman" because he only did lawn work and odd jobs.

"He was no problem," one of them said. "All he does is cut grass and make a little money."

Many neighbours described the police action as unnecessary.

"He didn't have a gun. All he had was a rake and he was at least 15 feet away, " said one.

"Their reaction was utterly ridiculous," said another neighbour. "There's no way in the world he could have attacked them."

"Their life wasn't in danger," a third neighbour said. "They could have maced him. They didn't have to shoot."

Police denied ignoring neighbours' and relatives' cries. They said they did not know Errol Shaw was a deaf mute.

In both instances, all police officers involved in the shootings were placed on leave with pay whilst internal investigations took place. All were exonerated for their actions.

At least in both cases, it could be argued police were responding to domestic disturbance situations and had to be on their guard. Thousands of miles away on the other side of the world, police officers in Chatsworth, near Durban in South Africa, did not even have that excuse. In a case that shocked many South Africans, four police officers were on trial for murder at the time the shootings took place in America.

The events that led to this started on 23 August 1998 when two police sergeants, Robinlall Baboolall and Pravesh Ramdeen, heard the sound of glass breaking and spotted a man acting suspiciously in the police station car park. As they approached him, they saw him drop flat to the ground behind Sergeant Ramdeen's car to try and hide from them.

Sergeant Baboolall picked the man up by his jacket whilst Sergeant Ramdeen inspected his car. Spotting a smashed window, Ramdeen saw that the man had his radio equaliser in his hand, apparently taken from his car. Furious, Sergeant Ramdeen slapped the man so hard on the back of the head as he was being hoisted to his feet that Sergeant Baboolall's the grip on his jacket was broken. This caused the man to slam his face on the hard surface flat, which resulted in a cut lip. Together, the two police sergeants hauled the suspect back onto his feet and frog-marched him roughly into the police station.

Ramdeen said later that the man had wiped blood from his wounded lip and the blood had splashed onto the wall. He had not cleaned up the blood splash but had left it to the cleaners to wipe down the wall.

After being frog-marched into the station, the man could not, or would not, walk any further so the two sergeants dumped him in a passageway, where the blood from his cut lip continued to drip onto the floor, whilst they went to open the charge room and make an entry in the records. The man was then dragged into the charge room and questioned.

Baboolall and Ramdeen testified in court two years later that it was only then that they realised the man was deaf and could not speak. He was then placed in a holding cell to await further questioning. Ramdeen and Baboolall then left the police station and attended to Ramdeen's damaged car. Ramdeen said this was the last time he had seen the suspect.

It was alleged in court that a short while after the man had been put into the cell that four policeman removed him and took him away for questioning about other cases. This lasted several hours, during which he was stripped naked and beaten so badly that the four officers had to fetch a supermarket trolley and load the suspect into it. As they wheeled him back to his cell, they were seen laughing aloud. Back in the cell, the prisoner was tipped head first out of the trolley and left lying on the floor. As an afterthought, one of the policemen threw a blanket over the man's naked body.

"He was placed in a cell and denied medical care," an investigator said later.

Sometime later, other policemen who had been too frightened to challenge the four officers noticed the man had not moved since being dumped in the cell, panicked and called an ambulance but it was too late, the man was pronounced dead by the ambulance crew. They still did not know his name!

It was only the next morning that a father called at the police station to report his son missing that the link was made with the dead man and the police were finally able to put a name to him. He was 22-year-old Clive Michael, who lived at Mariannhill, Durban. He had been deaf since birth and had a poor academic record. He was also destitute.

The incident was referred to the Independent Complaints Directorate, which had only been formed in April 1997 in response to years of concern about South African police methods. The unit was under-funded with only nine investigators to cover the whole of the KwaZulu Natal and Orange Free State provinces of South Africa, an area the approximately size of Austria. In the period between April 1997 and

December 1998, when the Clive Michael case was referred to the ICD, no fewer than 77 suspects had died in police custody.

The four police officers involved were arrested in March 2000 and released on ludicrously low bail of R5,000 by order of the High Court and continued to work as police officers! This led to furious protests by the Independent Complaints Inspectorate. "These men are dangerous," said an investigator. "Who knows what they may do next!"

However, an action by another judge led to a report being presented to the South African Minister of Safety and Security. "I am shocked," Judge Niles Dunier said, "that the Minister is unaware of widespread corruption at Chatsworth station." This resulted in a shake-up of the management of the police station, all of whom were deployed to other stations.

The trial began in November 2000 when Captain David Ragavan, Inspector Dhinasagren Govender and Constables Preganathan Naidoo and Collin Solomon appeared before Durban High Court accused of the murder of Clive Michael. All four policemen pleaded not guilty to the charges.

The prosecution alleged that all four officers were drunk at the time of the incident.

In his plea, Captain Ragavan said he believed that the injuries sustained by Michael happened when other officers were interrogating him prior to his own interrogation.

The prosecutor, State Advocate Santos Manilall told the court that Ragavan had booked Michael out of the holding cells so that he could be questioned about other possible cases. Michael had remained in the custody of these four officers until he was returned to his cell a few hours later.

In response, Defence Advocate Gideon Scheltema said this could not be proven because three registers relating to the incident were missing from the Chatsworth police station, to which the judge sarcastically replied: "Do you expect anything else from Chatsworth station?" implying that the reputation of the station was such that it was not to be trusted. Scheltema pointed to the missing registers as a "cover-up of epic proportions" as other officers had been involved in the death.

Cross-examining Sergeant Ramdeen, who was appearing as a witness for the prosecution and who had been granted immunity from any charges arising from the killing of Clive Michael, Scheltema put it to him that his own assault on Michael had been far more serious than a simple slap on the head. Ramdeen responded that he had only slapped Michael once, causing him to fall and that he had been surprised to learn Michael had later died in his cell. At the time of the arrest, he had not realised Michael could not speak and had thought he was simply acting. Ramdeen said he had followed police procedures by examining the cut on Michael's lip and filing a report for his superiors.

The case was adjourned for legal reasons and resumed in June 2001 in the same court. The first witness was Sergeant Baboolall who described how he and Sergeant Ramdeen had apprehended Clive Michael in Chatsworth police station car park after hearing the sound of breaking glass. He testified that Ramdeen had slapped Michael once in his anger upon finding his car damaged and a music system equaliser in Michael's hand. This had caused Michael to fall and cut his lip, which then bled profusely.

Baboolall testified that he had not been aware of Michael's disability until Ramdeen tried to question him. Once this was realised, he had left Michael squatting against a wall in the charge room and had no further contact with him.

Forensic pathologist partly corroborated the evidence of Baboolall and Ramdeen by testifying that the facial injuries sustained by Michael were consistent with a fall. He testified that the severe stomach injuries suffered by the prisoner were consistent with repeated heavy blows with a blunt object, such as a boot.

The case was then inexplicitly adjourned again after only two days in session, and had not yet returned to the court by the beginning of 2002, to the exasperation and dismay of the Independent Complaints Directorate and the victim's family.

In reality, the murder of Clive Michael had been the catalyst, which had exposed the vast corruption that had been going on at Chatsworth police station. For years, the station had gained a reputation as one of the most brutal, corrupt and incompetent police units in the whole of South Africa.

"Do you expect anything else from Chatsworth station?"

This acid comment from Acting Judge Shyam Gyanda in the first part of the trial of the four policemen accused of killing Clive Michael is fully justified when all the facts are considered. Prior to a massive shake-up at the station in April 2000 ordered by the Deputy President of the South African government, Chatsworth police station and its officers were involved in, or implicated in, or strongly suspected of the following crimes:

- The murder of Clive Michael in August 1998;
- The murder of a youth, Nasir Phili, in August 1999 during which three other youths arrested with him were repeatedly tortured and forced to lick the blood of Nasir Phili as well as their own;
- Being the perpetrators of South Africa's biggest armoured car robbery, the R32-million heist of the SBV cash transport company in Pinetown in 1997;
- Being involved in another R7-million cash-in-transit heist and other smaller robberies;
- Running several rackets demanding protection money from neighbourhood schools and businesses and issuing death threats against those who criticised those methods;
- Selling the station's guns and murder dockets for as little as R1E000;
- Accused of over-reaction to a brawl at a night club which led to the deaths of 13 partygoers;
- Implicated in other killings inside and outside of the police station, including that of Hoosen Shaik who was shot dead inside

the police station by Sergeant Hanujayam Mayadevan. The same police officer was also alleged to have distributed over R300,000 in cash bribes around the station to buy the silence of other policemen;

- Allegations made by South African President Thabo Mbeki that several police officers were responsible for the murder or assassination of other police officers to cover up massive corruption and criminal practices in the Chatsworth area.

Many Chatsworth police officers were also found to be living on income beyond what they should be reasonably earning as policemen.

In addition, Durban's senior prosecutor submitted a report to the National Directorate of Public Prosecutions urging action be taken against many corrupt officers.

The shake-up at Chatsworth police station resulted in 40% of all officers at the station being charged with various offences and many more being investigated as part of a police complaints probe. The entire management team was replaced, with officers being transferred to other stations.

The results of the shake-up were startling. In the three months before April 2000, less than 100 people were arrested for all offences; in the two weeks after the shake-up, a total of 355 arrests were made for crimes ranging from armed robbery to attempted murder and car hijacking and the station's reputation increased considerably.

"What has happened is that for the first time we have police actually doing their work. Before, we had a situation where the police themselves were committing the crimes," said the chair of the local police committee.

However, it remains to be seen if justice will be dealt to the corrupt and guilty police officers. Apart from the ongoing case relating to Clive Michael, where all the police officers involved are still on bail and still working as policemen:

- Five years after the R32-million robbery, no policeman has yet to be convicted;
- Three policemen facing murder charges relating to the death of one of a teenage gang of car thieves in August 1999 have still not had their case heard;
- No one has been disciplined for any of the irregularities with murder dockets or for their parts in the deaths of the 13 youngsters at the night club;
- No police officers have been charged with the alleged murders or killings of other police officers, or of other suspects killed in the police station like Hoosen Shaik.

Although there is still no satisfaction to the family of Clive Michael, they can be proud that the death of an insignificant, destitute, poorly educated Deaf young man has been the catalyst that has seen the break-up of a major police criminal gang and the subject of several major investigations into police corruption that led to direct intervention by the President of South Africa.

The Deaf Community will be watching to see if Clive Michael finally achieves justice.

Chapter 12

1998: Inverness, Scotland

Stabbed and Burnt

When colleagues at the British Bakeries depot in Burnett Road, Inverness in the Scottish Highlands noticed that Eric Innes had not turned up for work for two days, and had not even contacted their office with an explanation for his absence, they became concerned. An excellent and well-respected worker of 27 years service who was never late and always willing to do any overtime asked of him, it was most unlike him not to turn up for work or make contact if anything was wrong.

A colleague who was sent by the bakery at midday on Wednesday 23 September to investigate could not gain entry to the flat and the matter was reported to the police who were asked to investigate and make sure nothing serious was wrong. However, when the first police officers made their enquiries at the bakery worker's flat at 30 Friars Street, not far out of the town centre, they learnt that the person in question had not been seen for a couple of days. There was also a slight smell lingering in the hallway that resembled burning. After getting no answer to the doorbell, which was connected to a flashing light inside the flat to alert the Deaf occupant, the officers gained admission with a spare key held by the landlord.

Inside the flat, the smell of burning was much more obvious and investigating further, the officers found a body on the floor of the bedroom, and attempts had been made to set the room on fire.

By 3 p.m., an incident caravan had been set up outside the flat by officers of Northern Constabulary, which had its headquarters in the town and served the whole of the far north of Scotland. More than 40 officers were drafted in to assist with house-to-house inquiries.

The body, which had been unclothed, was too badly burnt for immediate identification but

Eric Innes

every indication pointed to the fact that the murder victim was the 5'2" slightly built Eric Innes, who only weighed just over seven stone.

Born in Portgordon, a fishing village on the Moray Firth about 40 miles east of Inverness, the victim had lived alone in Inverness for many years. He was a regular churchgoer and a strong supporter of the Highland Deaf Club, based at Kenneth Street, Inverness.

The post mortem results positively identified the body as Eric Innes from his dental records, and confirmed that he had been stabbed many times where he had lain on the floor and burnt after death. The post mortem also disclosed that the victim had been dead for at least 24-48 hours before the body was found.

Examination of the scene of the crime disclosed no signs of forced entry into the flat. The front door had been locked when police arrived and the presumption was that Eric Innes had either known his killer or had invited him into the flat.

Initial inquiries soon found that Innes had been last seen late on Monday night in several town centre public houses, a little drunk. Police discovered that his smartly dressed figure was well known in Inverness town centre pubs where he usually ordered a half-pint of lager.

This led to teams of detectives visiting all public houses and stopping people on the streets in a bid to jog people's memories. The police also confiscated all film going back 72 hours from all seventeen of the town centre's CCTV surveillance cameras, and several police officers were detailed the painstaking task of viewing all the footage.

This soon paid dividends when film footage was found of Eric Innes walking down Church Street from a pub and waving to another man and then the pair walking off together. It therefore became a priority for police to identify that man, either because he was one of the last persons to have seen Innes or it was the killer himself.

Because Eric Innes had been closely involved with the local Deaf community, police officers set up a textphone helpline in their headquarters and attended a meeting of the Highland Deaf Club where they were able to question those who knew the victim.

In order to widen access to Deaf people who might wish to contact them, the police also set up a web page on the Internet containing a special form for those who might prefer to contact them by email.

Police inquiries also disclosed that Eric Innes had a little-known secret, which not even his family were aware of. He was a homosexual. One theory about the killing, now that Innes' gay secret had come out, was that he had taken a man into his flat for the purposes of having sex. The position of the naked body on the floor of the flat lent to support this theory.

This disclosure prompted Reach Out Highland, a local sexual health charity, to offer to be the go-between to take confidential calls from members of the public unwilling to talk to the police because of their sexual orientation.

The murder also heightened security concerns amongst the town's pensioners and the local branch of Help the Aged charity were inundated with queries and referrals for the installation of spy-holes and security door chains.

Demand on the police resources and time became strained when there was another murder in the town on 27 September that needed the setting up of a second incident room and a second murder squad.

Help was sought from Interpol to trace a potential witness who had been travelling on a boat through the Caledonian Canal at the time of the murder, in case that witness had crucial information that would assist the investigation.

On 6 October, it was announced that door-to-door inquiries in all streets around Friars Street had drawn a blank. The same day, another announcement was made to the effect that all funeral donations would go to the local Deaf society.

Meanwhile, over in Lochgilphead, a town about 150 miles from Inverness on one of the West Coast lochs, a man was arrested for theft on 24 September, the day after Eric Innes' body had been found. He was a man with a long history of convictions for burglary and theft. Although he was questioned about possible involvement in the murder of Innes, it was to be over three weeks before he was identified as the man Eric Innes had waved to, and who was seen on CCTV walking off with the victim.

The police case against the arrested man became more solid when DNA extracted from blood found on articles, including knives, found in Eric Innes' flat was conclusively matched to him. On Monday 19 October, George McGeogh whose last known address was in Glasgow appeared in an Inverness court charged with the murder of Eric Innes.

When the accused came up for trial in February 1999 at Inverness High Court, it was soon abandoned when McGeogh dismissed his legal team and it was early September 1999, almost twelve months after the murder, that the trial finally got under way in the same High Court.

The jury of eight women and seven men listened impassively as evidence against McGeogh unfolded in the court over five days.

Detective Superintendent Charles Hepburn, who was in charge of the murder inquiry, described the murder as a despicable crime against a man who could not cry out for help. He described the investigation as one of the most intensive and significant investigations undertaken by the Northern Constabulary in recent years, requiring heavy use of manpower. He said that the investigation also involved three different forensic laboratories that all contributed to the mass of evidence that was built up against the killer, including the DNA specimens matching his profile.

DNA evidence crucial in trapping killer

THE investigation into the murder of deaf 61-year-old Eric Innes was the most intensive and significant enquiry carried out by Northern Constabulary in recent years, according to the man in charge of the case.

At the beginning of the investigation, Detective Superintendent Charles Hepburn described it as a despicable crime against a man who could not cry out for help.

And he claims that very good police work and the

By Lynne Illingworth

footage from videos in shops, railway stations and bus stations.

The help of Interpol was enlisted to trace a potential witness who had been travelling on a boat through the Caledonian Canal at the time of the murder.

"This is one of the most intensive and significant investigations this force has undertaken short of

home-room, a second set of enquiry teams and we got a result in both of them, the second one in 24 hours."

David Munro (33), of Lochiel Gardens, Inverness, was found suffering from serious head injuries on Sunday, 27th September, and died four days later. Teenager Derek Johnston has since been convicted of his murder.

who weighed 7 stone 4 and was 5ft 2ins tall, v brutal, according to I Supt Hepburn.

"There was certainly need for that level of v lence," he said. "Mr In was very, very light stature, but a fairly very popular man who w very well thought of at I work."

The fact that the bo was not found un Wednesday caused the o

The murder was well reported
in the Inverness Courier

The attack on Eric Innes, who weighted only 7 stone 4 lbs and was only 5 feet 2 inches tall was very brutal, according to the police officer.

"There was certainly no need for that level of violence," Hepburn told the court. "Mr. Innes was very, very light of stature although a fairly fit man. He was

126

also a very popular man who was well thought of at his work."

The fact that the body was not found until Wednesday caused the police serious problems, Hepburn said.

"We estimated we were three days behind the incident, so we had to backtrack his movements. There was no indication whatsoever that he had met anybody, spoken to anybody or had been in anybody's company."

The jury was shown the CCTV footage that had proved so crucial in securing an arrest in the investigation. Both Innes and McGeogh were clearly identified in the film footage. The court learnt that police had sifted through over 72 hours of film from the 17 CCTV cameras in the town centre, as well as footage from videos, shops, the railway station and the bus station.

Consultant pathologist Rosslyn Rankin told the court that a 14-centimetre wound to the neck that had punctured the jugular vein had caused death, resulting in Innes bleeding to death. This had been a blow of considerable force.

The victim had drunk enough to be three times over the legal drink-drive limit. He had been lying on his back on the floor when the fatal wound to the neck was inflicted. The victim has also sustained 13 injuries to his head and face. Six of these had been caused by blunt force, and smothering to the mouth caused the others.

George McGeogh said he had sustained a one-centimetre wound on his arm in the fracas in the fight, and claimed that he had been acting in self-defence. He said he had been invited for a drink at Eric Innes' flat after meeting him in the town centre and had fallen asleep in a chair.

He claimed he had been wakened by a naked Innes who had slapped him with a knife and gestured towards the bedroom. When he desisted, he had been head butted by Innes and the next thing he remembered, he was sitting in the bedroom where the body was lying near the bed. He then set light to the bedclothes to get rid of the evidence, and left the scene as soon as possible.

The jury unanimously rejected McGeogh's story, and took less than one hour to convict the 27-year-old Glasgow man.

The judge, Lord McLean, told McGeogh that life imprisonment was the only possible sentence that he could prescribe by law for the murder.

The court learnt that McGeogh had several pages of previous convictions. He had also earlier been found guilty and sentenced to three years imprisonment for trying to defeat the ends of justice.

Other charges to which he had pleaded guilty included theft and a breach of the peace in Lochgilphead where he had assaulted three police officers in trying to escape arrest. For these charges, and for trying to pervert the course of justice, McGeogh was sentenced to two years imprisonment, which would be served concurrently with the life sentence and the three-year sentence.

Chapter 13

1998: Limerick, Ireland

A Takeaway of Burger & Chips after A Takeaway of a Young Life

John Carroll had a hard life during his 21 years. Orphaned at the age of 12 when his mother died, he was fostered by a succession of foster parents until he was placed with Martin and Kathleen Quish in the village of Cappamore, Co. Tipperary, when he was aged 15. He was to remain with these foster parents for the next six years.

John Carroll

A fairly small man of only 5 feet 4 inches tall, he was of wiry build and an excellent footballer for his local team. He also loved disco dancing and would travel miles from his home to attend parties or other events. Born Deaf with a severe speech impediment, John also had a twin Deaf sister named Joanna as well as a brother Daniel, who had normal hearing. Sometimes they were fostered together, sometimes not. He attended a unit for deaf children at a secondary school in Limerick and after he left, obtained a temporary job in Limerick before securing a place in an upholstery-training course in the National Training Centre at Raheen, Limerick.

On the evening of 3 December 1998, he said goodbye to his foster parents in Cappamore, telling them he was going to Killaloe where there was a party in a pub. There, he met up with some people and accepted an invitation to accompany them back to a house where the party would continue. However, when he found that in order to stay the night, he would have to pay IR£30, he decided to leave.

His decision to leave set off a row with some of the other people he had accompanied to the house, and he was followed outside by several of them. One person who was well known for being violent still demanded the money. It was a dark night and it is well known deaf people cannot lipread in the dark, so there may have been communication difficulties. John Carroll still refused to pay so the other man who was demanding the money assaulted him by kicking him in the stomach, causing the unfortunate young man to fall to the ground, where he received further kicking about the body and the head by a number of other persons who had followed him outside.

He was then carried back to the house by some of the others and dumped on a couch where he apparently lost consciousness. It was clear he was seriously injured but the people partying in the house were too busy pleasuring themselves to bother with him. When he recovered consciousness about 15 minutes later, he was seen to draw '999' on the couch in blood with his finger.

A view of Killaloe,
where John Carroll spent his last night

A concerned woman who was in the house noticed this and became uneasy about what was happening.

"We better get him to hospital. Somebody had better call an ambulance," she said.

"Oh, he'll be alright. I'll take him in the car," said one of the men who had earlier assaulted him outside. With the help of the original assailant who had first demanded that John Carroll pay the IR£30, he was carried out of the house, followed by an 18-year-old girl whose babysitting shift in the house had ended when the group of people arrived. John Carroll was put into the back seat of the car which then left, and the other people went back to continue the party that had been so inconveniently interrupted.

But John Carroll never made it to the hospital. His badly beaten body was discovered by a farmer at 7.15 a.m. in a lonely country lane in a remote location near Ballinahinch, Co. Tipperary, over 30 miles from where he was last seen. He was lying in a foetal position in a pool of blood, dressed only in jeans, runner shoes and a thin blue tee shirt, which were totally inappropriate for the cold winter's night. The farmer who found him said a prayer over the dead body and put a covering over it before contacting the Gardai to report the finding.

It was not until the body had been removed for the post mortem that identification of the body was made through an identification wallet that was found inside his inner clothing and it was only a matter of time before the Gardai traced the last movements of John Carroll to the house in Killaloe where the party had been and began questioning the occupants.

The funeral of John Carroll took place the following week at St. John's Church in Cappamore, attended by a large representation of young people, both Deaf and hearing. Many were from the same training centre that John had attended and several wept as parish priest Father Michael Walshe spoke of John's gentle life and tragic death.

"Only this morning," Father Walshe told the gathered mourners, "I received a telephone call from a sports shop in Limerick. He was a regular there. He didn't spend much, but he was a great Chelsea supporter. The proprietors and staff there wanted to say what a nice, pleasant young man he was and how sorry they were that his life had ended so tragically."

John was mad about soccer, Father Walshe went on, and was an avid member of the Cappamore soccer club, and he idolised Chelsea. It was perhaps appropriate that John's body was laid out in his favourite Chelsea blue outfit.

He offered his and the congregation's condolences to John's brother and sister, and to his extended family of uncles and aunts and foster-parents Mr. and Mrs. Quish.

It was not until over two years later that the full details of how John Carroll came to meet his death were told in court, when a young woman named Deirdre Rose stood trial for his murder.

After being placed in the car to be taken to hospital, John had been mercilessly punched and beaten by a man sharing the back seat with him (the same man who had beaten him up outside the house in Killaloe). Instead of going to the hospital, the car with John Carroll and Mr. A in the back seat and a second man, Mr.B, behind the wheel drove aimlessly for miles whilst Mr. A tortured John Carroll at his leisure, despite his pleas to be left alone. In the front passenger seat, Deirdre Rose sat rigid facing forward, too scared of the violence to look back as Mr. A "... beat the shit out of him with his fists."

"Mr. A kept asking John for his bank card and PIN number. I knew we were not going to the hospital. I knew he was going to be robbed. I told him to search his pockets," Deirdre Rose said in a statement made to

133

police after she had been arrested on 5 December 1998.

Eventually, the car stopped in the lonely laneway near Ballinahinch and John Carroll was dragged out of the car. He was begging for mercy from his captors.

"Help me. Help me tell them leave me alone," John was reported to have screamed at the young woman.

"There is nothing I can do," she had told him and looked away.

John Carroll was then beaten on the head with an iron bar near his eye and the young woman could see blood going all over the place and one of the two men kicked him in the face.

"Watch the blood, lads," she called out to them.

"I knew at this stage that John Carroll was seriously injured. I did not tell either man to stop at any stage," she said in a statement read out to the Central Criminal Court in Dublin.

Finally, the two men decided they had enough of their sport and got back inside the car.

"Drive on," Mr. A told the other, "he's a dead man now."

"Is he really dead?" Deirdre Rose asked.

"He's a dead man for life."

After leaving John Carroll at the roadside, the three drove off and went to a fast food outlet where the two men ordered burgers and chips. The young woman just had a coke. They didn't mention the murder as they tucked into their food.

But John Carroll was not yet dead. When the three of them drove off, he was still alive and remained alive for some considerable time afterwards. He had a fractured skill, multiple injuries and had inhaled blood into his lungs. The Gardai thought it was possible that John Carroll had lived until just before the farmer found him. Officially, the time of death was placed as being somewhere between 9.30 p.m. on 3 December and 6.30 a.m. on 4 December, but investigators reckoned it was nearer 6.30 a.m.

Officially also, the cause of death was "blunt force trauma to the head" but hypothermia may have contributed to it. Deputy State Pathologist Dr. Marie Cassidy told the court that the deceased had severe head injuries that were "irreversible and irrevocable." Splinters from his skull fractures had been driven into the brain. There was also evidence of other blows to the head, to the ribs and the groin. Some of these were quite likely to have been caused by kicks.

State Prosecutor Eamon Leahy told the Dublin court that Deirdre Rose had been arrested on 5 December 1998 along with two other named men and charged at separate special weekend sittings of Limerick District Court with the murder of John Carroll after police enquiries in and around Killaloe had unearthed details of the fateful house party and pinpointed them as the last people to be seen with the deceased. After her arrest, Ms. Rose had made three voluntary statements to police officers detailing the events of the night.

The prosecutor put it to the jury that Deirdre Rose "knew from very early" on the evening that the intention was "rob John Carroll of money", not withstanding the fact he only had IR£30 on him.

"Deirdre Rose participated in that endeavour and encouraged the others as part of that to search his pockets. She said: 'Mind the blood, lads' as they set about killing him."

Leahy said that those engaged in a joint enterprise were responsible for the acts of each other and as such, Ms. Rose was charged with murder and assault with intent to rob. It did not matter that she had not participated in the actual assault.

Defence Counsel Brendan Grogan told the court that the defence accepted and admitted certain matters in the case, including the fact that statements made by the defendant were made voluntarily. However, he minded the court to note her own admission that she was a scared young girl of only 18, sitting in a car with a man offering gratuitous violence. She had admitted in her statement there was nothing she could have done to stop the violence.

Grogan told the court to consider the fact that Deirdre Rose was an 18-year-old woman who had never previously been in trouble. By her own admission, she had followed John Carroll and Mr. A out of the house where she had been babysitting in the first instance because she "didn't want anything bad to happen" knowing the reputation of Mr. A.

However, the jury only took three hours at the end of the three-day trial to return a verdict of guilty on the two counts of murder and assault with intent to rob.

Deirdre Rose, who was five months pregnant at the time of the trial, called out in anguish loudly from where she sat after the jury's verdicts had been read.

"What evidence have ye got that I murdered John Carroll? There was nothing that I could have done."

Mr. Justice Paul Carney invited her to say a few words more if she wished about the verdict.

"I'm sorry for all the trouble that happened but I murdered nobody. I robbed nobody. When you're afraid of a man like (Mr. A) who hurt people. He had an iron bar and was doing this and doing that. I was only 18 years old at the time. My baby is going to grow up with no mother and no father now that you have found me guilty of murder. Just think about that now," she told the jury.

Mr. Justice Carney thanked the jury for their service and told the court that he had never less understood somebody it had fallen to him to sentence.

"Ms. Rose has appeared in this trial as an attractive young girl who should have had a full life ahead of her. She was 18 at the time, is 20 now and had no previous convictions.

"All the material evidence was given by her and all her statements were accepted by the defence. The evidence was entirely of her authorship and it seemed that she acted with utter callousness and was totally indifferent to human suffering.

"The only issue in this case was whether she was present at these distressing events as a spectator or as a participant. The jury has answered in this manner."

Mr. Justice Carney told the court that the law left him with no alternative but to impose a sentence of penal servitude for life. He ruled that the sentence was to date from that day as she had previously been on bail.

Deirdre Rose wept as she was led away down to the cells to begin her life in prison.

Deirdre Rose on her way into court to be sentenced to life for her part in the killing of John Carroll.

But what about the other two men who were in the car with Deirdre Rose during the murder of John

Carroll, one of whom she had been so afraid of that she could not help?

The facts are that despite the statement by Superintendent Sean Corcoran, who was in charge of the investigation, to the press and to the court that there were further charges being considered at the moment in respect of the assault and murder of John Carroll, the two men still had not been brought to trial at the time of writing in January 2002, more than three years after the murder.

Mr. A:

This 22-year-old man from Limerick was charged at Limerick District Court on 5 December 1998 with the murder of John Carroll.

Murder accused further remanded

A Limerick man was further remanded in custody yesterday charged with the murder of a Co Tipperary man.

Before Limerick District

He is the man who it was alleged during the trial of Deirdre Rose to have set off the original beating outside the house in Killaloe; who had sat in the back seat of the car with John Carroll and hit him time and time again during that fatal journey; who had hit him with an iron bar in that lonely lane in Ballinahinch.

Mr. B:

This 24-year-old man from Killaloe was charged at Limerick District Court on Sunday 6 December 1998 that at Clarisford Moys, Killaloe on 4 December 1998, he falsely imprisoned John Carroll contrary to Section 15 of the Non-fatal Offences Against the Person Act (1997).

Both men must be presumed innocent until proven guilty by a higher court.

Chapter 14

1999: Melbourne, Australia

"Here's a daft idea; let's burgle the house of the son of Australia's biggest drug baron!"

Operation Phalanx was Australia's biggest-ever and most secretive police operation. It lasted eight years, produced over 600 intelligence reports, set up 16 separate police task forces, resulted in 135 arrests throughout Australia causing the seizure by police of eight tonnes of chemicals ready for production of amphetamines worth A$200 million, A$371,500 in cash, A$415,000 in forged US dollars, a farm used for drug manufacturing, and drugs (amphetamines, heroin, cannabis and cocaine) with a street value of millions of dollars. Also seized in the police raids were machineguns, hundreds of dollars worth of stolen property, vehicles and clothes. Other results included closing down three drugs 'factories', the discovery of twelve other discontinued drugs labs, seven lab sites and a chemical storage dump. It exposed an Australia-wide drug network with links to Thailand, Vietnam, Colombia, Hong Kong, and Amsterdam and severely damaged a massive Australian organised crime cartel.

It was also to lead to the life of a police informer and his family being completely ruined, forcing him to flee Australia and settle in Europe; to the discovery of corruption in one of Australia's elite police drug squads, the murder of one deaf person and a lifetime of fear for three other deaf persons.

141

It all began in the mid-1980s with a Hell's Angel motorcycle gang known as the Black Uhlans and a founding gang member named John William Samuel Higgs.

Born in 1946 and a habitual criminal since the age of 13, when he left school, Higgs had by the mid-1980s prior convictions for theft, assault, carnal knowledge, manslaughter, possessing cannabis and assaulting police. He was a gangster with a reputation for making enemies disappear and had been the target of a police operation since he had taken amphetamine production out of the hands of bikies. He was clever enough and well informed enough to avoid a major police operation that took five motorcycle gangs out of the drugs market, leaving him to monopolise Australia's drugs market. He recruited a failed New Zealand industrial chemistry student to produce top-class drugs on demand, stockpiled chemicals and held back hundreds of kilos of amphetamine drugs so that the market price remained high. To get an idea of how big a gangster he was, we have to look at the drugs world. People who deal with drugs on the street talk in grams; people who move and traffic in drugs talk in kilos but Higgs talked in *tonnes*. His influence and wealth was such that he was able to provide two hovercrafts to smuggle cannabis from Papua New Guinea into Australia's Northern Territory, from where it could then be moved down to Melbourne by one of the massive Road trains.

At one stage, Higgs had produced in one amphetamine production 'cook' street drugs with a value of A$48million.He owned land in Queensland valued A$18 million, an ocean-going trawler, a fish-processing plant and a shop in the Victorian town of Geelong. He could afford to lose $600,000 in a failed rock concert without even blinking.

As money rolled into his hands, Higgs employed accountants and advisers to try and launder the money and turn it into legitimate enterprises. He had mountains of money and was desperate to put it to use and make even more money, but this time legally.

In 1992, Higgs met a businessman in order to get an export licence to sell fish and stock feed to Asia and had made many overseas trips to set up business there. As the friendship, a mixture of business and socialising, between Higgs and the businessman developed, Higgs was helped to turn his money into legitimate business use. He freely admitted to the businessman his prior convictions for drug dealing

However, the businessman had friends on both sides of the law and had an acquaintance that was an investigator in the Bureau of Criminal Intelligence and the National Crime Authority. This policeman had been tracking Higgs for years and years, and had even arrested him once. However, Higgs and his gang had been one of the most difficult to infiltrate and get information about. They always managed to keep one step ahead of the law, and it was strongly suspected that Higgs had paid informers within the police drugs squad to keep him informed about police operations.

The policeman immediately recognised that the businessman represented the best opportunity the Australian police authorities had of getting inside Higgs' organisation and registered him as an intelligence source. The businessman was given the code name E2/92.

One day in 1993, Higgs paid a visit to E2/92's office and whilst the businessman was on the telephone, Higgs read some correspondence lying on the desk relating to a fertiliser deal with the chemical giant ICI. Higgs had recently fallen out with his chemical supplier in Sydney over a failed amphetamines cook, and thought that his friendship with E2/92 could prove a promising replacement. Within weeks, a gangland associate of Higgs arrived in E2/92's office and asked if he could provide bulk chemicals. This was typical of Higgs. He would not directly involve himself and use another gang member to set up the criminal activity.

E2/92 did not need to be an industrial chemist to be aware that he was being asked to become a partner in the amphetamine business and contacted his policeman friend. However, this friend was about to retire from the police force and arranged for E2/92 to meet in a North Melbourne coffee shop to discuss the matter with another police officer from the drug squad, named Wayne Strawhorn.

At that time, the drug squad had been probing Higgs and his network but was going nowhere after two years despite nine separate police operations into alleged drug dealing and murder. Only 11 days before Strawhorn met E2/92, the drug squad's head, Detective Chief Inspector John McKoy had written in a confidential report: "A concerted effort has been made to obtain a reliable informer against Higgs by targeting his known associates. To date detectives are no closer to charging him with drug matters than when we started."

E2/92 was a godsend for the police, but the initial meeting with Strawhorn was deliberately low-key. Nothing was written down and Strawhorn merely told E2/92 that he would be grateful for any information about Higgs and E2/92 simply said he would see what he could do.

The two police officers were concerned in one respect about E2/92. He was an amateur. In police undercover operations, the inside man is usually a police officer himself or herself who has been trained in covert operations and a volunteer who know at least what would be involved. For police, the safety of an undercover officer matters more than the operation. E2/92 was warned not to get out of his depth, as Higgs would have no hesitation in making him "disappear".

(It should be remembered that around this time the arm of a man later proved to be a known drug-dealer was found in the stomach of a shark caught off the eastern Australia coast. There is no proven connection with Higgs in this case, but it is an example of how people could be made to "disappear").

Years later, E2/92's wife would say: "I believe he was attracted to the thrill of police work."

But E2/92 took unbelievable risks and probably survived simply because he did not know what he was doing and relied on his ability to think on his feet. For example, he wore a tape to most meetings to gather evidence although discovery could mean certain death. One day, he had to meet a man later convicted for murder at midnight. After getting out of the car, he had a funny feeling and went back and ripped the tape out. When the other man met him, he said, "Someone's been lagging (giving information)," and took E2/92 to a deserted park and ordered him to strip to his underwear. Nothing was found and E2/92 survived to live another day.

There were other close shaves. One day, Strawhorn telephoned E2/92 when Higgs was in his office and listening in. E2/92 was able to pass Strawhorn off as the person who was obtaining the chemicals that Higgs was using to cook his amphetamines. Another time, one of Higgs' associates found a police bug behind the radio of his car, a car that had been supplied by E2/92. Only deft work by the police in stealing the car and removing the bug allied the associate's suspicions, he warned his boss, Higgs, E2/92 might be a police informer.

However, Higgs did not believe him because he was doing so well out of E2/92 and continued seeing him, making a lot more money in the process. Whenever the police raided Higgs, he would remain calm in the knowledge there would be nothing to connect him to any drug offences because he was so careful to make sure other people he employed in the gang did all the dirty work. To Higgs, police raids were an occupational hazard.

Higgs had escaped justice so long because he usually surrounded himself with family and friends he had known and trusted for years but his Achilles' heel was that he needed the E2/92's contacts in the chemical industry. What Higgs did not know was that the police themselves were supplying E2/92 with tonnes of chemicals. They gave the chemicals to E2/92 by the truckload, and E2/92 simply passed the chemicals on to Higgs. Even when members of Higgs' gang started getting arrested, Higgs refused to believe E2/92 was working for the police.

By early 1996, E2/92 was showing signs of the strain. He was speaking to Strawhorn almost every day, and there were persistent rumours going round that he was a police informer. When E2/92 first became involved, it was thought by the police he would merely be providing them with the odd piece of information but slowly the opposite had happened – he had become the pivot of the whole Operation Phalanx. Without him, there would be no case to answer for many of the players in the drugs scam.

E2/92 decided it was time to get out. One reason for this was that police had followed an associate named Krakouer delivering a load of amphetamines across to Western Australia in January 1994 and the Western Australian police had caught him red-handed unloading the amphetamines. Krakouer was sentenced to 16 years imprisonment, but his lawyers demanded a re-trial. In the process, they also demanded to see police documents leading up to the arrest and conviction. These documents named E2/92 as the informer and it was only a matter of time that the information would filter back to Higgs that his chemical supplier was not what he seemed to be.

E2/92 arranged to join the witness protection program. In Australia, the majority of those joining the program were criminals who had grassed on their mates or associates but E2/92 was unique. One

147

condition imposed by the Australian authorities was that E2/92 had to testify against Higgs in court.

E2/92 asked one simple question: "Will Higgs be convicted if I don't give evidence?"

"No."

E2/92 agreed to give evidence on the condition his family were protected. Given Higgs' contacts throughout Australia, it would have been impossible to afford E2/92 and his family this protection in Australia and police decided to send him out of the country. It was the first time Australian witness program authorities had relocated a key witness out of the country.

Even then, the authorities bungled the operation. They arrested Higgs before they all completed the negotiations needed to move E2/92 to a friendly country with a new identity, and he was forced to go on the run in Europe with his family. They had to severe all contacts with friends, other family members and everything in Australia, including their house and E2/92's business, which had earned him a comfortable A$150,000 per year. He felt betrayed by the authorities that had promised to protect him. They had dumped him without an identity, a future or even a country.

When Higgs realised the full extent of how police had snared him, his fury knew no bounds. To some extent, it was his own fault because he had been too greedy, buying chemicals from E2/92 at unrealistically low prices and treating him like a mug. Instead, he had found himself well and truly mugged.

John Higgs

He started to move heaven and earth to find E2/92, using his wealth to set out an enormous contract on the informer.

He also tried using his police contacts to try and find E2/92 and when this did not work (because the police had made sure that in order to prevent leaks, only people on a need-to-know basis knew where E2/92 was), he tried to bribe Strawhorn and another police officer with the staggering sum of A$250,000 each to get him documents and information leading to the whereabouts of E2/92. They refused the bribes.

Higgs knew that if he got rid of E2/92, the prosecution case would collapse.

With his Australian contacts having failed to locate his target, and two police officers refusing to accept bribes, Higgs resorted to another strategy. He paid other police officers to break into the electronically protected drug squad offices over Christmas 1996 where they stole files that contained more than 100 statements made by

John Higgs snapped in the street with one of his dealers
(police surveillance photo)

149

E2/92 and receipts and bills that gave away the witness' address, which at that time was an ordinary rented house in a small town near Manchester in England. It was there that the phone rang one morning at 3 a.m.

As soon as it rang, E2/92 knew it was trouble for only a few people knew where he lived. It was from the head of the Victorian police witness protection team and was short and to the point.

"You have to get out of the house immediately. You have been compromised."

The burglary on the drug squad's St. Kilda offices was one of the biggest security breaches in Australian police history and clearly was an inside job. A police statement later said: "It is the belief of the investigators that the most likely scenario is that between the 26 December 1996 and the 6 January 1997, the drug squad offices at the police complex,412 St. Kilda Road, Melbourne, were accessed by a member(s) of the police force, most probably by serving or ex-member(s) of the drug squad, who had an intimate knowledge of Operation Phalanx, and that member(s) removed the relevant documentation, and, at some later stage, handed the stolen documentation to Higgs in exchange for a substantial sum of money." It added that "security at the St. Kilda Road complex leaves a great deal to be desired."

E2/92 woke his wife, their two sons and his mother-in-law, who was visiting from Australia for Christmas. They packed hurriedly and ordered a cab to take them to Manchester's Piccadilly station where they caught the first early morning train to London.

From there, E2/92 and his family went on the run again in Europe whilst the mother-in-law returned to Australia. He would never know how close the family came to being exterminated by hit men contracted in Europe.

Having lost track of E2/92 in Europe, Higgs was forced to wait for his return to Australia to testify in the forthcoming court case. When he did, E2/92's movements were under close surveillance as murder plot after murder plot was hatched to prevent his testifying. At one stage, two motorcycles were deployed against the car in which E2/92 was transported daily to and from court with armed pillion riders who would blast the car as they drew alongside, a method favoured especially by drug gangs in Colombia.

However, police security was extremely tight and Higgs' associates failed time and time again to carry out the hit.

At one stage during court proceedings, the prosecution were granted a magistrate's order to have E2/92 testify over a video link rather than transport him to and from court each day, and eventually, John William Samuel Higgs was sentenced to six years imprisonment for his part in the amphetamines business, with an order that a minimum of four years had to be served before parole could be considered.

Despite being foiled time and time again, Higgs did not give up trying to exact his revenge against E2/92 who had left Australia as soon as he had given evidence. He contracted other accomplices in Australia to discover E2/92's new whereabouts and over the Easter break in 2000, the offices of a Melbourne lawyer, Paul Duggan, were burgled. It was an unusual burglary in that the thieves ignored cash and valuables lying around, but hacked into the computer, broke open a filing cabinet and took with them a dictaphone, a mobile phone and computer disks containing information downloaded from the hacked computer. When they left, the thieves locked the door behind them.

It was clearly a new attempt to discover E2/92's whereabouts because Paul Duggan was his lawyer and also because E2/92 was still giving evidence in other cases that had involved Higgs' associates.

It was not just Higgs and his associates who went down in the drugs bust. Ongoing investigations into corruption within the Victoria police drug squad had led to several dismissals and convictions as well through undercover sting operations. There was also one death of a police officer that was very suspicious. Another drug squad detective, living in the Melbourne suburb of Hoppers Crossing (a name that would crop up later), was killed along with his wife and two sons in a suspicious head-on car crash in December 1995.

Such was the extent of Higgs' Australia-wide drugs network that repercussions were still being felt two years after he had been sent to jail. Some of these now affected the Melbourne Deaf Community.

John William Samuel Higgs had a son, Craig, who was aged 35 at the time his father was sentenced to his six-year term of imprisonment. Deaf from birth and educated at Victoria School for Deaf Children, St. Kilda Road, Melbourne, Craig Higgs had followed his father into the drugs trade and was well known to the police.

The Victorian School for Deaf Children, Melbourne
where Craig Higgs was educated

At the time of his father's imprisonment, Craig Higgs was living in a luxurious home in the Melbourne suburb of Hoppers Crossing with his second wife, Sonya, who was also Deaf. Craig had previously been married to a Mandy Florini, a hearing child of deaf parents, and had three children by her.

Within Melbourne's Deaf Community where he was well known although he did not attend the local Deaf club much, Craig Higgs was a man you walked around on eggshells because of his father's connections and strong rumours persisted that he was heavily involved in drug dealing. In fact, he was regarded as the main supplier to Deaf drug users, and had started supplying drugs to his friends while still at school! Obviously, with all the publicity surrounding the trial of his father, many of the rumours took on the form of Chinese whispers, becoming more and more exaggerated as they passed from Deaf person to Deaf person. First it was alleged that a large amount of amphetamines rolled up like a salami and weighing about 1 kilogram fell out of a shopping bag inside his kitchen, then it was alleged that a roll of money was seen lying openly on the top of a television cabinet in his lounge.

At first, it was said that the money roll contained A$28,000. Later it became A$50,000 and the size of the money increased as rumours built on rumours until some people believed that there was at least A$40 million hidden in a wardrobe in the bedroom shared by Craig Higgs and Sonya.

This improbable tale was believed by a group of young Deaf people. After all, they reasoned, only a small proportion of Craig's jailed father's drugs money had been found by police – just A$350-odd thousand. Where was the rest of the estimated A$120 million that all the newspapers were talking about? What were the odds that some of that loot was being looked after by Craig Higgs? After all, his new home at Hoppers Crossing was probably built with the proceeds of drug money.

One young Deaf man, 20-year-old Benjamin Masters, excitedly bragged to one of his friends he was going to get his hands on that A$40 million and if Craig Higgs resisted, he would get hurt.

"Don't be so bloody stupid!" his friend told him, possibly possessing more sense and more awareness of what would happen if the money did get stolen from

Craig Higgs. His father might be in prison, but that did not mean he was not capable of ordering his associates to take revenge against anyone who crossed him.

But Benjamin Masters would not listen. Once the idea had taken hold of him, it just grew and grew. Craig Higgs and his wife were a soft target. They were deaf so would not hear the break-in, and all being well, they would just sleep through the burglary. The only other occupants of the house would be their three small children who could easily be dealt with. He sold the idea of doing the burglary to two of his deaf friends and a hearing friend who all seemed to think it was a good idea.

So, at 2.30 a.m. on the night of 7 December 1999, the four of them broke into Craig Higgs' home armed with metal pipes. The only woman among them, 21-year-old Chelsey Campbell, was detailed to stand guard in the children's bedroom and make sure they did not wake up and intervene in the burglary.

The other three, Masters, his Deaf friend David Northern aged 24, and hearing accomplice, 18-year-old James Caffery, crept to the parents' bedroom where Craig and Sonya lay asleep.

In their incompetence, they awoke the sleeping pair and instead of being cowered, Craig Higgs fought back. In the panic, both Masters and Caffery hit out wildly with their metal pipes, whilst Northern, unnerved by the violence, fled the house.

The Higgses were both left bloodied with fractured skulls as the two men fled the house, collecting Chelsey Campbell on the way out. They had achieved nothing. They had not time to find any money and the sum result of their bungled burglary was to leave two adults seriously injured.

The noise of the struggle woke up Craig Higgs' eldest son, 12-year-old Jan, who went to investigate, switching on the lights to find his stepmother walking dazed, blood pouring down from her head wounds. The two other children in the house, both girls aged seven and five, were terrified and traumatised when they saw what had happened. Sonya Higgs managed to convey in sign language two words, 'scared' and 'hurt'. It was Jan who telephoned the Higgs' natural enemy, the police, for help and Melbourne's Armed Offenders Squad responded promptly. After all, the name of Higgs was well known.

Craig Higgs was flown by helicopter to Melbourne's Alfred Hospital where he was operated upon and put on a life support machine. This was switched off the next day when he was declared brain dead. Meanwhile, Sonya Higgs was rushed to the Western General Hospital where she was reported to be in a serious condition.

It was a senior policeman who went to the prison where John Higgs was being held and told him quietly in a private room that intruders had murdered his Deaf son in a burglary attempt. It is not difficult to guess how Australia's amphetamines king reacted to the news of his son's murder and the threat to his grandchildren. Clearly, police had to get to the burglars before his associates did.

It did not take long either for the Deaf Community to react to the murder of Craig Higgs or for fingers to start pointing at Benjamin Masters who had been bragging about his intent to burgle the house. He was soon arrested and it was not difficult for police to get from him the names of his accomplices. Northern, Campbell and Caffery were all quickly arrested.

They were all charged with murder, aggravated burglary and intentionally and recklessly causing serious injury, and remanded in custody. They all pleaded not guilty to the charges.

Sonya Higgs recovered from her injuries in hospital and was soon released but the prosecution case received a serious setback when she subsequently received serious head injuries when a car slammed into the driver's side of her own car. This left her in a vegetable state. There were rumours that her brake cable had been cut so she was unable to stop at a road junction. The accident was alleged to have been set up so that she would be prevented from giving evidence as a witness in the court case.

When the preliminary hearing at Melbourne Magistrates Court was finally able to get under way in June 2000, the prosecution informed the court that Sonya Higgs was unlikely to ever be able to give evidence and formally requested that her statement given in hospital after the incident be withdrawn from evidence.

In the preliminary hearing, several Deaf witnesses told the court through relays of sign language interpreters about how it was rumoured in the Deaf community that Craig Higgs kept drugs and huge rolls of cash in his Hoppers Crossing house. One witness testified that Benjamin Masters had cried after the killing when he admitted that he and James Caffery had been responsible for the bashing that Craig and Sonya Higgs had received.

The court also heard from Chelsey Campbell that she was told by Masters prior to the burglary she had to stand guard in the children's bedroom and hit them with her metal pipe if they woke up.

"Ben said if the children wake up, just hit them once and knock them out," she told the court. She denied that she had any intention of using the steel pipe on them.

Magistrate Peter Mealy bailed Campbell and Northern to appear in the Supreme Court in October, but remanded Masters and Caffery, as the only accused who had taken part in the bashings, in custody.

However, it was not until February 2001 when the four defendants appeared in court. In the meantime, through plea bargaining, all four had changed their pleas from not guilty of murder, to guilty of manslaughter.

It was packed with members of Melbourne's Deaf Community who followed the proceedings vividly through sign language interpreters. They saw Masters and Caffery also plead guilty to the charge of recklessly causing serious injury to Sonya Higgs. The prosecution told the court that Mrs. Higgs was still unable to make a victim impact statement due to the injuries she had received from the car accident.

The court heard that Mr. and Mrs. Higgs had woken up to be confronted by stocking-masked raiders looking for drugs and rumoured millions of Australian dollars in cash. In the fight that followed, the two Higgs were severely bashed with steel bars by two of the raiders who had fled empty-handed. Both were very seriously injured and Craig Higgs had died the next day in hospital. Their three children had been traumatised by the incident.

Benjamin Masters was said to have a mental age of a 14-year-old and was also dyslexic which had affected his education. His counsel, Stratton Langslow, told the court that thanks to television cartoons, Masters believed that people who were bashed with steel bars would completely recover.

The court heard that Chelsey Campbell was influenced by Masters to take part in the raid. Although she had not taken part in the bashings of the Deaf couple, she had admitted she had been prepared to hit any of the children with a steel bar if they woke up during the raid.

The counsel for David Northern told the court that he had gone along with the raid naively believing that he would come out of it a wealthy man. He had not expected the violence that erupted and had fled the scene, abandoning the others still in the house.

Justice Bernard Teague accepted the defendants' guilty pleas but deferred sentencing for reports until April 2001.

In his sentencing speech, Justice Teague remarked that the appalling crime committed by such unlikely criminals had made his task a very difficult one due to several factors. He called the four defendants naïve and gullible due to their deafness, and in the case of the normally hearing Caffery, to his youth and sheltered upbringing.

"Unfortunately, a substantial degree of naivety typically affects people suffering from a profound hearing loss from birth. No person with a normal balance of trust and scepticism would be likely to believe that a family man would keep millions of dollars in his bedroom wardrobe," he told the court, however adding, "I do not believe that the disability of deafness can be treated as a medical condition warranting any significant moderation to the principle of general deterrence."

The judge said he would take into account the difficulties that profound deafness would cause Masters, Northern and Campbell in prison.

"Vulnerability to the predatory acts of other prisoners is potentially much higher for deaf prisoners than for prisoners with hearing," he said.

There was another matter that was causing him a great deal of concern, he told the court. The victim's father, he said, was a man of considerable means and clout in the criminal world and was in prison himself.

"There is an understandable perception that Mr. Higgs' father would be displeased about the killing of his son," Justice Teague told the defendants.

There was no doubt that all the four defendants were right to be fearful of what would happen to them in prison and for this reason, the judge would be making an order that all the defendants should be placed in protective custody during their time in prison.

He sentenced Benjamin Masters to a maximum of seven-and-a-half years' jail with a non-parole period of four years for his role as planner of the raid, and for his part in the bashings.

James Caffery was sentenced to a maximum jail term of four years, with a non-parole period of two years for his part in the burglary and killing.

The judge accepted that David Northern had fled the scene when the violence had erupted but nonetheless he was still guilty of manslaughter. He was jailed for three years but advised that he could apply for parole in four months.

Chelsey Campbell was sentenced to a maximum term of three years and ordered to serve a minimum of six months in prison. The judge said that although she had not struck any blows, she had been prepared to hit any of the children if they woke up.

Supreme Court Justice Teague's comment about Craig Higgs' father being "displeased" about the murder of his son is perhaps a massive understatement. If John William Samuel Higgs was prepared to:

- ❏ Put out a contract on E2/92;
- ❏ Pursue E2/92 to Europe and hire European hit men to kill him in Manchester;
- ❏ Plot to murder him on his return to Australia, including two hit men to ride as motorcycle pillion passengers and shoot at his police escort;
- ❏ Offer A$250,000 bribes to two drug squad detectives to 'lose' documentation relating to his offences;
- ❏ Bribe other drug squad members (or ex-members) to burgle the drug squad offices

and remove all the paperwork relating to his offences and try to discover E2/92's whereabouts;

❑ Arrange for the offices of E2/92's solicitors to be burgled;

how much would he pay to avenge the death of his Deaf son?

By the police's own admission, John William Samuel Higgs had a reputation for making people disappear.

Perhaps Benjamin Masters, James Caffrey, David Northern and Chelsey Campbell might be safe in prison because of protective custody but how long would any of them last when they got released from prison before they became another "disappeared" statistic?

Chapter 15

2000: Bishop's Stortford, England

Case Unsolved: Death in an Alleyway

Partially deaf since early childhood, 34-year-old Scott Newman was fairly well known in the small town of Bishop's Stortford, Hertfordshire. It was not just because he was deaf and easily recognised by the hearing aids he wore on both ears; it was also because he frequently used different pubs and clubs in the town where he was known to indulge in his bisexual activities. In spite of this, Scott Newman was a well-liked young man who liked to have a laugh with people.

The Falcon public house where Scott Newman lived and
did an occasional shift behind the bar

He was close to his family, especially his divorced mother and sister who lived in Bishop's Stortford, but lived on his own in a room in the Falcon public house in the centre of Bishop's Stortford. His father and a brother lived in Cambridge.

Following an education at Tewin Water School for Partially Hearing Children in Welwyn Garden City, Scott Newman held down three different jobs. Apart from occasional work behind the bar in the Falcon pub where he lived, he was also employed as a cleaner on an industrial estate on the outskirts of the town and as a petrol attendant at Welcome Break's Birchanger Services on the M11 motorway. Before that, he had worked at several filling stations around the town including Budgen's Supermarket.

Scott Newman spent the evening the evening of Sunday 9 July 2000 drinking with friends at the Falcon pub. Since he lived on the premises, he had "a lock-in" after the pub closed for the night.

As midnight approached, he told his friends he was feeling a little hungry and would go and get a takeaway meal for himself.

"I'll have to get some money first," he told his friends as he examined his wallet to see if he had enough cash to purchase his takeaway.

An examination of his financial records would later confirm that he withdrew £20 cash from the Nationwide cashpoint in South Street around midnight. That was the last point at which his movements could be pinpointed.

His body was found by a passer-by in a pedestrian alleyway off the town's Riverside Walk at 2.25 a.m. the next morning. After the police were called, Scott Newman was pronounced dead at the scene by doctors and taken to the Princess Alexandra Hospital at Harlow where a post-mortem was performed. This determined that a blow to the back of the head had killed him with a blunt instrument. There were other bruises found on his face but these were believed to have been caused when he fell after being struck. He was not robbed; his wallet containing cash and credit cards were found on him, and no possessions were missing although he was wearing only one hearing aid instead of the normal two.

A murder enquiry team of 60 officers, codenamed Operation Aestival, was set up under the direction of Detective Superintendent Bob Saunders who established an incident room in the refurbished police station in Basbow Lane. The superintendent said in a statement to newspaper reporters that the crime was unusual.

"There has to be a specific reason for this attack. It's an extremely rare type of attack for such a safe town," he said. Many of the officers were studying footage from closed circuit television cameras, including those from Marks & Spencers and the fast food outlet, Kebabery, both of which might show people entering Riverside Walk.

The alleyway where his body was found was strewn with old bricks and broken concrete bollards. These were removed by police for forensic testing.

DS Saunders appealed for a young white woman aged approximately 25-30 who was seen in Riverside Walk in the early hours of Sunday morning to contact the police. He described her as a "vital witness."

Two weeks after the murder, the police revealed they had found evidence a sexual act had taken place in the alleyway where the murder had taken place, but refused to disclose whether the sexual act had involved Scott Newman himself.

"The alleyway is an ideal location for sexual activities. It is out of the way and out of the line of sight from anywhere," Detective Superintendent Saunders told reporters in a new interview. There was also a public toilet nearby which was a favourite pick-up spot for gay and bisexual men looking for anonymous sex.

He refused to disclose exact details of how the 34-year-old partially deaf man was killed or left in the alleyway.

"This is something only the killer would know," he said, adding that investigating officers were awaiting detailed forensic evidence that could provide clues to the killer's identity. This included growing DNA samples that could take up to 20 weeks to complete.

The next day, 27 July 2000, police announced they had made a major breakthrough with the arrest of a local man who would be charged with the murder of Scott Newman.

Nine months later, in March 2001, it was apparent the murder investigation was at a stand-still, with no new developments taking place. The much heralded "major breakthrough" and "arrest" had not led anywhere; no person had been brought to court charged with Scott Newman's murder and now, one of the deceased's friends, Andy Barnes, who had also worked and lived in the Falcon public house, announced that he was to run in the forthcoming London Marathon in aid of the charity Defeating Deafness.

Postscript: At the time of writing (January 2002), there have been no further developments in the Scott Newman case. Hertfordshire police describe the murder inquiry as "ongoing" and refuse to divulge any further details.

Acknowledgements

Several people have been of great assistance during the writing and research of this book. Some, for professional and personal reasons, prefer to remain anonymous.

I would like to thank my wife Maureen for her assistance in every step of the way, from research to help with the text layout.

Several friends and acquaintances overseas have been very patient with me in researching and pinpointing sources. In particular, Bernard Le Maire (Belgium), John Lovett (Australia), Francine Della-Catena and Carla Williams (both USA) and David Breslin (Ireland) have been very helpful.

Anthony Boyce, Geoffrey Eagling and Raymond Lee of the British Deaf History Society have been helpful in contributing material and photographs.

We have tried to trace copyright holders of all pictures used but apologise if we have inadvertently contravened any existing copyright.

Acknowledgements and thanks are due to the *Los Angeles Times,* the *Limerick Leader* and the *Leicester Mercury* for permission to use their photographs.

Index